THE MAKING OF
KING KONG

The Official Guide to the Motion Picture

Jenny Wake

Motion Picture Screenplay by Fran Walsh & Philippa Boyens & Peter Jackson
Based on a story by Merian C. Cooper and Edgar Wallace

POCKET BOOKS
New York London Toronto Sydney

POCKET BOOKS, a division of Simon & Schuster, Inc.
1230 Avenue of the Americas, New York, NY 10020

Unit photography by Pierre Vinet. Provided by and © 2005 Universal Studios.
Photographs on p. 20 of Jeremy Bennett and Gus Hunter © Matt Mueller & Iva Lenard.

ISBN-13: 978-1-4165-2867-8
ISBN-10: 1-4165-2867-9

This Pocket Books trade paperback edition February 2006

10 9 8 7 6 5 4 3 2 1

POCKET and colophon are registered trademarks of
Simon & Schuster, Inc.

Designed by Ruth Lee Mui

Manufactured in the United States of America

CONTENTS

Filmmaker Peter Jackson.

One night, when Peter Jackson was nine years old, he saw the original *King Kong* in flickering black and gray on television. The classic movie made him cry—and set him on the path to a brilliant film career.

"That moment of seeing *King Kong* was the moment I decided I wanted to become a filmmaker," says the multi-award-winning director, thirty-four years later. "I wanted to do what the makers of *King Kong* did. I wanted to bring to life stories and adventures and creatures that couldn't possibly be done any other way than through making a movie."

It is late afternoon on an autumn day, 2005, in Wellington, New Zealand, and postproduction on Peter's remake of *King Kong* is in full swing. He snatches a few moments between meetings to lie back on the window seat in the farmhouse-style kitchen at the headquarters of WingNut Films (the production company he co-owns with screenwriter Fran Walsh) and reflect on the magic of the original *King Kong*.

"It was the perfect piece of escapism," he says. "When I was nine, it swept me away. I was transported into this amazing world and this adventure." Central to the adventure was Kong, the giant ape, portrayed initially as a monster but bit by bit transformed into a sympathetic creature. "I was sobbing by the time Kong died at the end of the movie. It was the perfect blend of mysterious adventure with a story that touched your heart.

"People go to the movies for different reasons, and everybody is different in what they like and dislike. I love escapism. I think movies should let you experience things that you can't experience in your real life, and going to a lost island and finding it inhabited by dinosaurs and a huge gorilla—to me, that was just the perfect escapist entertainment."

The original *King Kong* was made in 1933 by Ernest B. Schoedsack and Merian C. Cooper. It starred Fay Wray as the beauty who captures the hearts of both the beast Kong and the sailor Jack Driscoll, played by Bruce Cabot. In the 1930s, America was in the grips of the Great Depression. The Empire State Building had just opened, little was known about mountain gorillas, and animation was in its infancy. *King Kong* wowed Depression-era audiences with its savage beasts and derring-do and has continued to move audiences to tears through the decades.

King Kong's monsters were created by special effects genius Willis O'Brien. O'Brien had pioneered a technique known as stop-motion animation, for which he filmed creature models one frame at a time, repositioning them slightly between each exposure. When the film was played

A VISIONARY FILMMAKER

back at normal speed, the creatures appeared to be moving. O'Brien's Kong stood eighteen inches tall. It had a steel skeleton with ball-and-socket joints. It was padded with foam rubber and covered with rabbit fur. Frame by frame, it battled dinosaurs with thrilling ferocity, ruthlessly dashed sailors and hapless New Yorkers to their deaths, fell hopelessly in love with young actress Ann Darrow, and made a heroic last stand against civilization from the top of New York's Empire State Building.

To today's audiences, accustomed to digital effects, O'Brien's pioneering stop-motion animation looks quaintly artificial, yet Kong still springs to life as a character. "The power of the original *King Kong* didn't dwell in how realistic the effects are. It's the magic of the film," says Peter. "It's the sum of all the parts. It doesn't matter that you can see the magician performing the tricks. It's the quality of the tricks that has the effect on you."

Being able to see how the magic was done on *King Kong* allowed Peter to have a go at it himself. "In a way, the artifice is still what's exciting about stop-motion. It excites you about the possibilities of filmmaking. You're bringing inanimate objects to life and you can invest them with a personality. Certainly it was possible even as a kid to do the same thing. There are a huge number of filmmakers, special effects people, makeup artists, who owe their careers to the original *King Kong*. That one movie has, I think, started more people on a career in filmmaking than any other film ever."

Peter's own first steps toward a film career involved lots of plasticine and his parents' Super 8 movie camera. At age nine, inspired by *King Kong*, he started sculpting dinosaurs and other little monsters and moving them around. For a year or two he experimented with the camera and made various short Super 8 films.

Then he hatched a plan to actually remake *King Kong*. "I would have been about twelve or thirteen by that time. I made a model of King Kong, for which I used a fur stole that my mother had in her wardrobe. I'd never seen her wear it in my whole life, so I managed to get her to part with it, and I trimmed off the fur. I made a little rubber King Kong with wire inside him, and I glued on the fur off Mum's fur stole. I made a cardboard model of the top of the Empire State Building, and my mum donated an old bedsheet, which I painted. I stretched it out and pinned it up on a board and I painted a backdrop of the Manhattan skyline. I put my Empire State Building in front of it and did a little bit of stop-motion animation with Kong. I started to do a little bit of jungle too. I made some plastic trees and I had a little stop-motion plasticine brontosaurus sort of grazing on the trees.

"I didn't get very far. The filming took a long, long time to do, but was probably no more than thirty or forty seconds. I had a lot of fun building the models, but I realized that trying to do a remake of *King Kong* was a little bit ambitious. I still have that film somewhere. I haven't seen it for years, but I've got all of my old films in a box. And I have that Kong. He's very deteriorated now, but he's still in one piece."

Throughout his teenage years, Peter dreamed of someday becoming a special effects man. "I didn't really have any ambitions to be a director as such," he says. "I guess I didn't really know what directors did when I was young, but I knew what special effects guys did, so for a long time I wanted to do stop-motion as a career. But then, as I did little tests and made short movies, I realized that a lot of the fun is making up ideas for stories and telling stories through film and learning how the camera angles and the cutting all go together to make a movie. I realized that the most fun is if you direct the movie, and that a career in being a special effects person would ultimately be a bit frustrating because I wouldn't be telling the stories that I wanted to do. So it took me till I was in my twenties before I realized that being a director was what I really wanted to do."

Peter's first feature film was *Bad Taste*, a hilariously grisly horror-comedy about aliens set on harvesting fresh human meat for their intergalactic fast-food franchise. It was filmed on weekends over four years, with a handful of Peter's best friends acting as cast and crew. Peter, who was working as a photo engraver for a local newspaper at the time, saved every cent he could to buy film stock and materials and made his own props, special effects makeup, camera rigs, and pretty much everything else he needed, in his parents' garage. Eventually the New Zealand Film Commission provided funding for postproduction, and in 1988 *Bad Taste* splattered onto screens around the world, starting with the Cannes Film Festival.

"Peter is a very unique director because he has

Richard Taylor with Peter Jackson on the set of *King Kong*.

never had to serve his time on other people's film sets," says Richard Taylor, Peter's longtime friend and business partner. "He decided one day he'd become a film director and so became a film director."

Richard and Peter first met when Peter was directing *Bad Taste* and Richard was working as a model-maker on a television commercial. By chance, a mutual friend invited Peter to visit during production of the commercial. "I had heard rumors of this filmmaker up in Pukerua Bay making this alien movie, so I went over and chatted to him," says Richard. The meeting would ultimately lead to career partnerships, award-winning movies, and the fulfillment of dreams.

At that time, Richard and his partner Tania Rodger were building puppets in the back room of their home and dreaming of one day creating a substantial special effects facility. "Over the next years

Tania and I spent much time in Peter's company . . . every evening we'd spend time together talking about Ray Harryhausen movies, and talking about *King Kong* a lot."

Richard and Tania provided puppets, miniatures, and gore effects for Peter's next movies, *Meet the Feebles* and *Braindead* (aka *Dead Alive*). Their friendship led in 1994 to the formation of Weta, the award-winning special effects company co-owned by Richard, Tania, Peter, and film editor Jamie Selkirk. With the release of *Heavenly Creatures*, *Forgotten Silver*, and *The Frighteners*, Weta grew and diversified into the realm of digital effects, eventually becoming two companies, Weta Workshop and Weta Digital.

"Making films is our passion," says Richard, "so we will build the facilities we need for a particular film, as much as we can afford to, by mortgaging everything else again to get the facilities built. We

1996 Triceratops creature concept by Christian Rivers.

1996 Kong face study, ready for mold making.

want to get the films made at the best level we can, so we grin and bear it, hang on for dear life."

It was Universal Studios that initially came to Peter with the idea of doing *King Kong*. "In 1996 we were halfway through *The Frighteners*," recalls Peter. "An executive at Universal who was working with us on *The Frighteners* suddenly called one day and said that they were looking at properties that the studio owned that they wanted to develop in the future and did we have any interest in some of their ideas. He mentioned two or three titles and one was *King Kong*. I nearly fell off my chair!" Peter laughs. "I said, 'It's my favorite film! You really want to do a version of *King Kong*? Wow! Yeah, sure!'"

Peter and his partners swung into action. Peter and Fran wrote a script, and Richard and Tania contracted extra staff. "We hired a fairly large crew," says Richard Taylor. "We invested in more digital equip

Dominic Taylor fine-tunes a pneumatic Kong hand mechanism in 1996.

ment, set up the facility here at the workshop ready to take on the body of work, and launched into the design and preproduction phase."

Bernie Wrightson, American comic-book artist, creature designer, and illustrator, flew to Wellington to help conceptualize the world of Kong and Skull Island. "We did hundreds of illustrations, and dozens and dozens of conceptual sculptures, designing around Kong and the creatures," says Richard. "It was a very delightful and enjoyable time. We were on our first big international feature film and there was a great feeling of euphoria and excitement."

To bring the creatures of Skull Island to life, the plan was to use a combination of stop-motion animation, animatronics, and digital effects. Stop-animation armatures were built for the brontosaurs, tyrannosaurs, Kong, and the raptors and fleshed out with foam latex. Animatronic versions of their heads were planned for close-ups, and work began on a full-size animatronic creature. "In the original script, there was an attack on Sumatra by some giant crocodiles," says Richard, "and we had started sculpting a full-size body and head for this sequence."

A large-scale miniature of the whole of Skull Island was built, from which other miniatures were being planned. Visual effects teams at Weta Digital were working on dinosaur walk cycles, researching techniques for creating Kong's fur, and modeling the whole of New York digitally, building by building.

Six months into preproduction, Universal Studios shelved the plan to remake King Kong, after a string of monster movies underperformed at the box office.

As he remembers it, it was three thirty on a Tuesday afternoon when Fran Walsh phoned Weta Workshop with the bad news. Richard recalls, "Pete was with Fran, but was too upset, so Fran called us on his behalf. I went down to the workshop, gathered the crew together, and told them. There were tears and sadness. We felt that we had finally got our chance to prove ourselves and do an international picture of great esteem, and to have lost it was desperate for us at the time."

Most worrying was how to find employment for all the digital artists who had been contracted to work on the project for the next two years. Thankfully, director Robert Zemeckis, who had earlier teamed with Peter and his partners for *The Frighteners*, offered Weta Digital some effects work on the movie *Contact*. "That was a great grace and let us move on," says Richard. "But all credit to Universal, because they stayed with Pete, watched *The Lord of the Rings* unfold, and came back with *King Kong* when the time was more right. They were correct ultimately—we did need to let it go [at that time]. We firmly believe we can do a beautiful job of it today, where I question if we could have back then."

With *King Kong* on the shelf, Peter turned his attention to securing a studio deal to turn J. R. R. Tolkien's trilogy, *The Lord of the Rings*, into a series of movies. In December 2001, *The Lord of the Rings: The Fellowship of the Ring* premiered worldwide to critical acclaim and blockbuster box-office success, as did *The Lord of the Rings: The Two Towers* in December 2002, and *The Lord of the Rings: The Return of the King* in 2003. The trilogy won multiple awards for Peter, Fran, Richard, and others who worked on the films, and catapulted Peter to the very top of Hollywood's A-list of directors.

"It was really Universal killing our 1996 version of *Kong* that propelled us into *The Lord of the Rings*—which in hindsight was obviously a good thing," says Peter, laughing. "We've ended up making everything in the right order, so in a funny kind of way fate's been kind to us. Coming back to *King Kong* now, we've been able to apply everything we learnt from *Lord of the Rings* as filmmakers, and so it's a better time to make *King Kong* now than it would have been in 1996."

The entrance to Weta Workshop.

The Lord of the Rings trilogy took seven and a half years to make, giving Peter and his partners the opportunity to develop a stronger infrastructural base for their moviemaking empire initially based at Camperdown Studios.

Camperdown is a rambling set of interconnected buildings with a colorful history that Richard can recite in great detail, right down to the spot where his mum's lawyer's wife was born. It was a derelict site when Richard and Tania, out for a bike ride, spotted the For Sale sign. It had been a pharmaceutical factory ten years earlier and, before that, a battery factory, a GI intern hospital, and a psychiatric hospital. The friends bought the building for a song. It would turn out to be a first step toward developing all the resources they would eventually need to produce films as big as *King Kong* or *The Lord of the Rings* trilogy.

The quiet suburb of Miramar, Wellington, seems an unlikely setting for a complete collection of cutting-edge film facilities, but is now home to Weta Workshop, Weta Digital, Stone Street Studios, a motion capture stage, Weta Productions (a television production arm), Weta Collectibles, Weta Tenzan Chain Maille (a chain mail manufacturing company), and Weta Publishing. The most recent additions to the film facilities dotted around Miramar include Park Road Post—a state-of-the-art postproduction facility designed and lavishly decorated in the style of architect Frank Lloyd Wright—and a massive new soundstage, dubbed Kong Stage, at Stone Street Studios.

"Today we feel much more adequate to realize a great piece of American pop culture in a suitable way," says Richard. "We've learnt a lot since 1996. Half of our careers have passed since then. We've grown up, and Peter's got greater clarity on what he saw the world of Kong to be. The script is tighter and more dynamic. We've grown more mature and longer

12

Peter Jackson behind the camera.

in the tooth, so we feel that we can bring a much more sophisticated level of design to it."

The version of *King Kong* now in production is radically different from the version that would have been made in 1996. "It was a very simple action-adventure film," says Peter. "It had some of the action sequences that we have today; it didn't very have much of the character development. It didn't have much going on in its heart. . . . It was very over-the-top, and it reveled in its outrageousness in a way. For the film that we're making now, we completely rewrote the script.

"There's no doubt that *The Lord of the Rings* had a huge influence on the way that we ultimately rewrote *Kong*, by making it a little bit more real at its heart, making the characters more real, and making the dynamics between characters more centered and more focused. One lesson that we learnt with *The Lord of the Rings* was that the best way to tackle fantasy is to make it as realistic as you possibly can. No matter what the fantasy is, make the characters and emotions as real as they can be. Our 1996 *King Kong* knew it was a fantasy film and didn't make any attempt to be real."

That's not to say that the 2005 *King Kong* will delve into heavier themes. "We didn't want to over-invest it with too much baggage, too many messages and themes and weighty stuff," Peter says. "There aren't very many what I'd call old-fashioned action-adventures made anymore now. And that's what *King Kong* is—it's sheer escapist entertainment. You can go watch the movie and be swept away to another place, another time, for two hours."

Peter regrets that youngsters no longer watch older classics such as the original *King Kong*. "There is a generation of kids today who have very little patience for watching a film that's in black and white, and of course, *King Kong* has got old effects and old styles of scriptwriting and acting. So to take that great story and to remake it so that it's accessible to kids, I think is a good thing to do.

"The original film will still be there. There's nothing that we're doing that's going to threaten the original film. It's a classic film and will always remain so."

Perhaps with the rise of a new generation of filmmakers, there will be some who say they are making movies because they were inspired by Peter Jackson's *King Kong*. If so, Peter will be delighted: "There is that continuum which I think is very important. You're hoping when you make films that there's some nine- or ten-year-old kid out there who's going to become a filmmaker in twenty years because of the film that you've made."

For now, though, Peter's focus is simply on making a movie that he himself would love to see. "But I'm not so much making this film for the adult me," he says. "I'm making it for the Peter that was nine years old once, who for the first time saw the original *King Kong*."

An early exterior design concept of Kong's lair by Gus Hunter.

Even as Peter Jackson, Fran Walsh, and Philippa Boyens raced to complete *The Return of the King* and get their early ideas for the *King Kong* script down on paper, concept illustrations started pouring out.

"We didn't have much of a brief at that stage," says conceptual designer Gus Hunter. "I would do artwork and it would be sent in a package to Peter, and he would have a look at it over the weekend. I think at that time we were taking bits and pieces of the 1996 *King Kong* script—knowing that it would be changed, but it was a place to start. Now and again we would get dribs and drabs of feedback through Richard Taylor, and he'd say, 'Pete's quite happy, do some more.' So I'd carry on, just immerse myself and have fun."

A key conceptual design focus was formulating the look of Skull Island: "What does the jungle look like? I was really blown away by the original when I was a young chap, and I got the movie out again and watched it a few times," says Gus. "The real task was trying to re-create the Skull Island of the original movie, but have Peter's feel to it."

Peter loves the stylized look of the 1933 movie. It harkens back to the fantastic biblical and literary illustrations of Gustave Doré, a nineteenth-century French illustrator whose work inspires artists and filmmakers to this day.

CREATING SKULL ISLAND

"Gustave Doré," explains Richard Taylor, "had a particular style where he lit environments with an immensely strong central light on the central figure, whether that be Moses or Christ or whoever, and then allowed the outside of the frame to drop away to a very dark tone, creating visually stunning and filmic images a long time before film was ever invented. The technique that Willis O'Brien and Marcel Delgado used to do the special effects for the original *King Kong* complemented this sort of artwork, and it made for very beautiful filmmaking, on a par with movies made today."

The special effects scenes in the 1933 *King Kong* were filmed using a layering technique. A typical jungle shot might have live or miniature foliage in the foreground, several clear sheets of plate glass framed with painted vines and foliage in the middle ground, more three-dimensional foliage between each sheet of glass, and a matte painting or previously filmed stop-animation footage back-projected onto a large translucent screen in the background. The dark foregrounds, midtoned middle grounds, and bright, pale backgrounds created an illusion of great depth and distance, with the actors highlighted in the midground.

"There was a certain look to the original film where you went from dark to light

An older study by Jeremy Bennett of the Brontosaurs.

Above: Early design concept by Gus Hunter showing Skull Island's tortured coastline and broken landscape as seen from a distance.
Below: A painting by Jeremy Bennett, taking a previz frame and extrapolating on it to create a creepy feeling for the swamp.

Below: One of a series of studies by Jeremy Bennett of the Brontosaur stampede environment.

to dark to light," says conceptual designer Jeremy Bennett. "There was a nice tunnel-like effect with the old glass matte paintings—these wonderful silhouettes with vines and things, taking advantage of the smoky, brighter backgrounds."

Gus Hunter.

"In a way it's quite simple, how they did it in those days," says Gus.

"It's very simple, but I've actually found it surprisingly difficult to replicate," says Jeremy, laughing.

Jeremy Bennett.

Once preproduction for *King Kong* was in full swing, Gus and Jeremy produced conceptual paintings at an average of four each per day. Sometimes it ultimately took as many as seventy paintings to capture the essence of a single Skull Island environment. They were joined for a time by Alan Lee, preproduction conceptual artist, at the tail end of his involvement on *The Lord of the Rings*. Alan produced many beautiful concept drawings for Skull Island, and his ideas for the village had a direct influence on the layout of this huge set piece. Gus and Jeremy worked independently of each other and met with Peter twice a week.

"Peter always said, 'I'd prefer if you guys actually didn't look at each other's work,'" says Jeremy. "So come Friday, I had no idea what Gus had done, and he had no idea what I had done, or how many we'd each done. We'd be pinning them up, looking over our shoulders at the other guy's work—so nerve-racking, because you just wanted to crack a design for something."

An environment study by Jeremy Bennett illustrating the journey from the coast to the village.

Arrival at Cairo of Prisoners of Minich, by Gustave Doré.

"But it was good," says Gus, "because there were two different styles. . . . [Peter] would choose bits and pieces of both our artwork and he would tell us to do a second pass at it. And we'd meet back after three days. We'd refine it until we had it. Sometimes we'd be lucky and hit it straight off, but that was very rare."

Left: An early study of the wall by Jeremy Bennett. "I imagined the gate totally blocked with debris: tree trunks, rocks, anything they could set their hands on," says Jeremy. Right: An early study of the New York docks by Jeremy Bennett.

"Peter's incredibly positive," says Jeremy. "He's very good at telling you what he likes and why. It's very rare that you come away feeling brutally critiqued. But you just want him to like it so they can move ahead and start building things, because everyone's waiting on you.

"In some areas he would have a really clear idea. He would even draw something on the whiteboard. Other times he'd just say, 'Come back in a couple of days and show me what you've got.' . . . Pete knows exactly what he's after. He won't sign off until he gets it. You might show him a painting that he'll really like, and he might not change anything about the idea, but the composition—the placement of stuff—he might have a few notes on, and he's always right. . . . And in that sense I really enjoy working with him because his aesthetic is so refined."

The ancient architecture of Skull Island presented a special challenge to the conceptual designers: "It couldn't be any architecture that anyone has seen before," says Gus. "We had to do a lot of concepts of what the wall was going to look like. Pete didn't want the ancient-civilization architecture to be too sophisticated."

"It wasn't like the Aztecs or the Mayans at the height of their civilization, for example," says Jeremy. "Not as advanced. If you look at the structure of the wall and what it was built from, it's monumental in its size but it doesn't have the finish of dressed stone by the Egyptians. You can put a credit card through the cracks of the blocks—it's not an Incan masterpiece."

New York, being an existing city, did not require much in the way of conceptual design. "We did a bit of painting on the look of the dock area," says Jeremy. "We've always got a dark shape—whether it's ropes or a bit of a crane or crates—in the foreground, so we've managed to find ways of duplicating the basic composition from the original here as well."

Over at Stone Street Studios, the art department's concept room is wallpapered with Jeremy's and Gus's paintings. In Weta Workshop's miniatures studio, where sculptors are carving Skull Island landscapes, concept paintings are skewered to blocks of polystyrene and scattered over workbenches. The concept designs form the basis for the construction of live-action jungle sets, miniatures, and digital

Conceptual art: Brontosaurus grazing environment.

Conceptual art by Gus Hunter illustrating an ancient overgrown city within the Island, which has become a lush grazing area for the Brontosaurs.
Inset: Previz shot of Brontosaur environment. The previz was done before the concept art.

backdrops and give everyone a clear sense of the look and mood Peter wants for each setting.

In the final weeks of principal photography, Jeremy and Gus are still hard at it. "We're now fully immersed in the visual effects, which is all the blue-screen stuff," says Gus. "We're designing the matte paintings for the matte painters."

"Which is good fun," adds Jeremy, "because we're almost having a second pass at those environ-

ments now—you can clean them up or refine them, and anything you might have missed, or an aesthetic that may have evolved a little bit, you can now advance."

"Watching the shots now coming together, they are starting to look so beautiful and so evocative and so filmic," says Richard Taylor. "For me, Peter has found a wonderful balance between the very fantastical and a very gritty, very harsh, very real world."

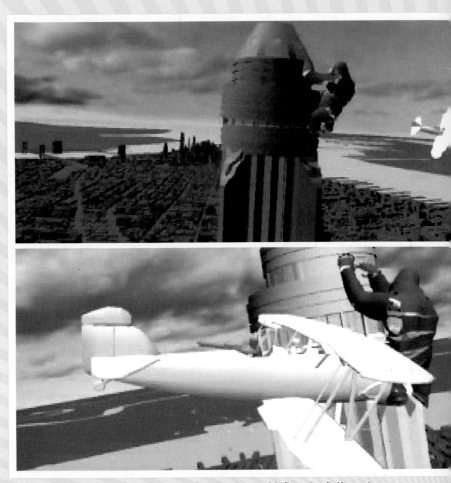

Frames from the previz of the Empire State Building attack.

On Richard Frances-Moore's computer screen there is a rough animation of Kong in shades of gray. All around him are the shapes of Times Square—vehicles, theaters, people. Kong whirls around, confused and disoriented. He knocks over a car, his frustration building. The animation lacks color, sound, and any kind of detail, but the dynamics of the action tell the story: a desperate Kong is embarking on a destructive rampage through the streets of New York.

Richard is a lead animator at Weta Digital. The scene on his screen is a previsualization animatic, more commonly referred to as previz.

"Previz," explains Richard, "is using computer animation to do the storyboarding—the visual development of the film, shot by shot, before anything gets shot on set. It's a tool for Peter to be able to say, 'This is what I want the scene to look like.' It's an extension of storyboarding. For Kong we haven't done any [traditional] storyboarding at all."

Previsualization director Christian Rivers used to be a storyboard artist, most recently on The Lord of the Rings. "Peter would describe the shots for the film and I'd sketch them," he says. "Now we have a team of people, and rather than storyboard it, we discuss the scenes and the action and we animate in 3D—fairly roughly, but accurate to the broad strokes of what Peter wants."

The first scenes the previz team tackled were for the film's final sequence at the Empire State Building. "The script was still loose," says Richard, "but they knew they had to have Kong and the Empire State Building, so that's where we started."

"I think the Empire State Building sequence really brought a lot of people into what the film was going to be like," says lead animator Andrew Calder. "Initially when you come and work on *King Kong*, you think, 'Big adventure movie, silly monsters'— whereas the Empire State Building sequence has quite an impact. It's serious and tragic, and a lot of people really responded to it, even in previz form. It really sets the tone: 'Oh, *this* is the film we're working on.'"

Armed with conceptual artwork and a brief from Peter, the previz team starts each scene by developing choreography for the action. Kong's battle with the V-Rexes has evolved into a nine-minute sequence, but in the script it was just a few words long: "It was 'Kong fights three V-Rexes. *Rarrr!* Battle ensues,'" says Christian, laughing. "There was no time limit on it. Peter said, 'You've got three V-Rexes, you've got Kong, you've got Ann, you've got a jungle, come up with some ideas.' So we spent a bit of time just giving him some crazy options. He picked ideas that he liked, and they ran through his filter and then came back out in the sequence order that they now stand in the film."

PREVIZ

For many scenes, the previz human characters were animated using motion capture, whereby a live actor's movements are captured on computer. Long before the start of principal photography and the arrival of the actors on set, Christian, Peter Jackson, production assistant Mike Wallis, and animation director Eric Leighton performed most of the human characters on the motion-capture stage.

"We started using motion capture to quickly get humans that we could throw into the scene and interact with our big beasties," says Eric Leighton. "So we all dressed up in Velcro and spandex mocap suits with little dots all over ourselves, and we performed all of the roles. I did a lot of Jimmy and Hayes, Christian did a lot of Adrien's stuff, Pete did lots of Denham, and we all danced around and threw ourselves on the ground and hit invisible bugs."

The beauty of 3D animation is that, once the previz artists have roughed out a sequence of action, it can be viewed from any direction as if through virtual cameras. In that respect, it is just like live action: one can choreograph the action and then set up cameras to film it from particular angles.

"We would animate the previz just looking through one particular virtual camera, like standing back wide and watching it all happen," says Christian. "And then Pete says, 'Okay, yeah, I like what they're doing there, now give me a camera where we start in low, a close-up on the rex, and swing the camera around while Kong sweeps through frame.' So then you follow certain actions as if you were a cameraman, and it gives the whole sequence a really natural dynamic that sometimes isn't there in visual effects shots because they're composed and so meticulously engineered."

Once the previz artists have generated the raw footage—the close-ups, the wide shots, the low angles—it is all handed over to Peter and editor Jamie Selkirk, who do a final selection of shots and then edit the footage together, essentially providing a rough cut of the scene before the cameras even start rolling.

Previz is the roughest of animations, and yet it communicates a surprising amount of information. Peter has used it every day on set to show the crew and the actors what he has in mind for each scene. It can also be played back on a "video assist" monitor with the live action superimposed, so that Peter can make sure that the actors are appropriately positioned in relation to the computer-generated elements in each shot.

The previz cut of each sequence will also be used as "a tool for planning the visual effects, and by every other department," says visual effects supervisor Ben

Left: Previz of the Brontosaur stampede. Information is burnt into each frame: 866 is the frame number; (24 - 981) is the frame range for the sequence; Lens: 28mm is virtual camera information which is important for the camera units; 123 is the scene number; 043 is the shot number. The sbs number is an internal previz number. Right: Previz shot for Kong's fight against the V-Rexes.

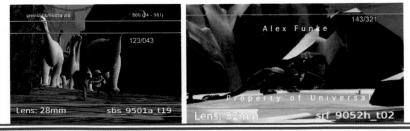

Skull Island - Kong Capture at Wall - 163/017

Top left inset shot is the previz image, which was created first. Below it is Jeremy Bennett's concept art for Kong's capture. Here we see Kong leaping in pursuit of Ann and Jack. This study was done for the miniatures and digital departments.

Snow. "The art department will use this information to help create the sets. If the second unit is shooting some material, then Peter will use these to explain to the second unit director the sorts of elements that he wants. And the previz helps Miniatures and Workshop plan what sort of models to build and how they should be shot."

"We build a whole 3D environment for the previz," explains Christian. "For instance, we'll design a terrain for where Kong is fighting, and Weta Workshop will build pretty much the terrain to match that."

At a later stage of production, the previz team goes into a kind of postviz phase, combining live-action footage with tidied-up previz, to give the digital and miniatures teams more specific and up-to-date information they can use in finishing the effects shots.

As the previz artists animate their way at breakneck speed through the movie, they are very much at the hub of the production, helping Peter to tell the story of *King Kong*. "All the people who do previz have to have a good sense of storytelling and how to move a camera to tell a story," says Richard. "It's a jack-of-all-trades, master of none."

Top: Macy's building in Herald Square, dressed with Christmas decorations. Left: Construction phase of the Burlesque Theater. Right: The Burlesque Theater is redressed as the Princess Theater for a later scene. Opposite page: Burlesque Theater architectural plan (blueprint).

Rather than find filming locations and turn back time in present-day New York, the *King Kong* production team decided to re-create several blocks of thirties-era New York on a vacant site in Seaview, an industrial suburb just a twenty-minute drive from downtown Wellington.

Wellington is a hilly city, with a reputation for winds that occasionally howl up to gale force, and finding a flat, sheltered site large enough for New York proved to be impossible. The Seaview site is flat, at least, but is surrounded by fuel-storage tanks and exposed to the cold winds that whip across Wellington's harbor.

"Believe me, we looked all over Wellington not to choose that space, because we knew how exposed it was," says producer and first assistant director Carolynne Cunningham. "But there

was nothing that was flat enough, big enough, and had the facilities around it to be able to put in all the trucks and the unit people and everything that's required. So we got stuck out there in the middle of the fuel tanks, with emergency procedures in place in case something went boom.

"It was such a big set and the art department worked like Trojans to get it done," she says. "They had rain, they had wind, they had everything that could possibly slow them down."

The script required settings for Times Square, Herald Square, a low-rent district, and a variety of streets in different parts of the city. Fortunately, Times Square and Herald Square have similar layouts with Broadway cutting diagonally through each, so a plan was hatched to build Times Square with

NEW YORK, WELLINGTON

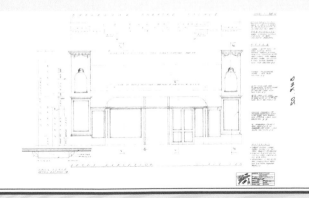

30

part of Broadway, Seventh Avenue, and several cross streets, then transform it midshoot to Herald Square on Sixth Avenue. Running parallel to the avenue was a road lined with typical tenement buildings, dubbed Tenement Street. It catered to the very opening sequence of the film, a scene-setting series of vignettes of life in 1930s New York.

"New York was big. New York takes the cake in terms of big sets," says Dan Hennah, supervising art director. "The site was just big enough to accommodate it. The expectation was winds in excess of one hundred kilometers an hour, so we used our good old reliable container technology."

"Container technology" is the ingenious use of walls of shipping containers to anchor building facades so they won't topple or fly away in a gale. The huge green or blue screens, used where the background will need to be replaced by a digital environment or backdrop, can also be supported by walls of containers. The short streets and avenues of the New York set dead-end in green screens.

"You can hire a container for two bucks a day," says construction supervisor Ed Mulholland. "So it's a cheap, very strong option for putting up the screens, rather than doing a big scaffolding work. It's all engineer-approved. If you look behind the set of New York, you'll see we've put a lot of containers down, put twenty ton of water barrels in them to counterweight them, and then tied the back of the set off to the containers—basically using the containers as a huge weight to hold the set together."

Accordingly, the theaters, shops, and tenement buildings lining the streets of New York are just one story high. "Our sets are all two containers high, which is five meters," says production designer Grant Major, "so there was a five-meter limit to all the sets we built—which happily is pretty much where the street level stuff and the tops of the canopies finished. And then everything above that will be digitally

added in. That's a job I'm doing for Weta Digital at the moment—going round all the sets that we built and identifying the building type and textures and signs that will go on all those extended pieces."

Once Weta Digital's visual effects wizards have worked their magic, New York's skyscrapers will look tall and the avenues long, but the streets and buildings around the two squares may look a little skinnier than usual. "We scaled our New York sets down by about twenty percent," Grant says. "We just didn't have the space and the budget to build it full scale, but through a camera lens I don't think you'd ever know."

Other than the reduction in scale, extraordinary efforts were made to match the look of 1930s New York. To that end, a team of researchers sought out every accessible photographic record of the period to serve as a design guide.

"It's been almost two years of extensive research," says researcher Sarah Milnes. "New York was so different from what it is now. We concentrated mainly on the buildings to start off with, just getting a general look, but then it goes down to small details like

Mid-construction/painting phase on a corner of Times Square.

what was the window frame made out of, or what color was the original. All the photos are in black and white so it was quite hard to tell what colors things were.

"We found a lot of stuff on the Internet, accessing the New York Public Library online and e-mailing or phoning research librarians over there—or an expert in shipping or theatrical productions. And if you get the information from one source, you've got to back it up from somewhere else."

The research team also ferreted out photographs and information about the inhabitants of New York and the day-to-day details of their lives. "We looked at how people were living," says Sarah, "how much things cost, what sort of work people were doing, the food that they would eat, their general lifestyle and living conditions, the soup lines, the protests, what sort of things they would protest about, what signs they would have; also the ethnic makeup of New York, what socioeconomic groups would be in certain areas, and then things like costumes—small bits and pieces on every aspect."

After studying New York for two years, Sarah went out to the set during filming. "It makes your hair stand on end," she says. "It's a little bit creepy because it's so real. You take photos on set and convert them to black and white, and they look exactly like some of those original pictures."

The walls of Grant Major's office in the art department at Stone Street Studios are papered with floor plans, color charts, and photographs of New York, including one of Times Square. A movie sign in a photograph pinpoints the date it was taken as April 1933. "It's one of our prime reference photographs," he says. "It has many of the shops that we copied. We also did a people count of that photograph to judge how many extras we'd need on any given day. Per block, I think there were one hundred and fifty-five people in that shot. And we counted vehicles on the street.

"We copied a lot of the signage. We wanted to get it exactly right. When you look at any of the photographs, it's a sea of signage—not just advertising material, but a lot of civic stuff, right down to park

Peter Jackson walks the streets of New York City.

Kalamazoo Diner in downtown New York City.

ing signs and street signage—a huge amount of detail. We had six graphic artists working for months and months on all that, and a similar number of sign writers. And then we had quite a few electric signs—on the theater canopies in Times Square in particular."

Grant is adamant that faithfully re-creating the finest details of period photographs is worth the effort. "The more you look into these photographs, the more fantastic detail there is," he says. "Truth is stranger than fiction in some ways, and the truth of these photographs is far more interesting than what you can conjure up in your mind as a fantasy version of it. . . . And also we want to make Americans, particularly New Yorkers, feel comfortable with the whole thing. There'd be nothing worse than them getting into this movie and then not believing their New York. Gritty realism is what I was after—in all its casualness and its busyness."

The gritty reality of the New York set was that it took hundreds of people months to build it. "We threw people at it," says Dan Hennah. "We had the site for six months, so we had a bit of time, but when we were busy trying to get other sets ready, we kept stealing people off New York and pushing them into other sets, so it was a bit of a push to get New York ready at the end. But it was always going to be, to get the degree of detail and authenticity that we felt it warranted."

The roads were laid early on in the building schedule so that, over time, they would be weathered by sun and rain, and the dirt tracked over them by construction vehicles. "Peter was very keen on the gritty, textural look to everything," says Grant. "All the period photos of the times show a lot of litter on the streets, and the streets didn't have the money spent on them so they were starting to degrade. So that suited us, from that gritty point of view and also from the

Barber shop and hardware store on New York City street.

budget point of view. There was a delicate balance between the money we had to spend and the look we were after and the period fidelity we wanted."

"We poured all our own curbing and pavements, and all our own cobblestones," says Dan, "but we had roading contractors lay the major tar seal for the rest of the streets. . . . And then we added a huge amount of old newspapers and cabbage leaves and dry autumn leaves."

Railway contractors installed the rails for the tram. "That was something we didn't want to take any risks with," says Dan. "We had a real tram, but we didn't have the resources to put in an electric rail, so we put in a piece of steel channel with a chain in it, and we put a winch on the tram so that it winched itself up and down the chain. The chain didn't move, but the tram did. It was a background

thing to a large degree, but it was a great element to have, because it's such a big-scale piece that even peripherally it helps with the illusion that you are in New York."

The job of pumping steam out of manholes on the streets fell to the special effects team, who laid nearly two kilometers of piping under the roads. "We had a couple of big boilers and each outlet was individually controlled," says special effects coordinator Steve Ingram, "so if one outlet was where they wanted the camera, it could be turned right down, or you could pump more steam out of the ones in deep background."

Getting the underground pipes laid out for the steam system turned into a nightmare job. The site is at sea level, so the team immediately ran up against the water table. As fast as they dug plumbing

The special effects team makes artificial snow.

Burlesque Theater lit and ready for shooting a night scene.

trenches, the holes filled up with water. To add to the problem, there was constant rain.

"There was so much water that the steam pipes wouldn't get up to temperature," Steve explains, "because they were being cooled by the water they were sitting in. We had to dig those bits up again and encase them in concrete so the water couldn't get to them. It was a huge job, but we got it. We had seventy-odd steam sources plumbed in there, all individually controlled, and it worked really well."

Steve's team also trimmed the streets with piles of snow. "Peter's idea was that when it had snowed, it

was dirty," Steve says. "It had been cleaned out of someone's doorway and thrown into piles with the rubbish and dirt, and it didn't make the city look beautiful."

Five thousand sacks of bark mulch—ground-up bark—were used to bulk and shape the snow piles. Each heap of bark was covered with a layer of Dacron, and insulation foam was sprayed over the Dacron, forming a hard crust. Around the edges the special effects team sprinkled Epsom salts, which glistened under the lighting.

Stairs to nowhere and ten steel support pillars were all that was built of the station and elevated

A wide shot of Times Square. A lighting tower is affixed on the top of the set for night shoots. The hills in the background will be replaced with digital New York City images.

track for the el system. The topless pillars, standing in pairs, marked the route of the absent train track. "It started off snaking from Broadway, then we took it away altogether for some shots, and then we brought it back in and ran it all the way down the avenue as part of the Herald Square setup," says Dan Hennah. "It took three men twenty minutes to move one of those pillars."

Eight engineers worked full-time for months building lampposts, street signs, and wrought-iron fences. A team of sculptors carved the decorative moldings for every building facade out of polystyrene. Set finishers textured, painted, and dirtied-down exterior surfaces and painted marblelike flooring in entranceways. Props buyers and props makers supplied merchandise for every shop, and set dressers arranged them in the windows.

"I had twenty-odd people there," says supervising set dresser Tanea Chapman. "We gave each dresser eight shops to take care of, so for us it was an opportunity to have a little bit of creative freedom. . . . Grant walked round with me and said roughly what he wanted: 'This is a shoe shop, it'll have a stand of shoes. This will be a restaurant.' The great thing about having so many people doing shops side by side [is that] it did look quite gen-

The Lyric Vaudeville Theater where Ann performs, dressed and ready for shooting.

uinely like different people had done their own window display, which is what window dressing is all about."

At times the art department swelled to almost the man power required for *The Lord of the Rings*. "When we were majorly stretched with New York, we had 475 to 500 people in the art department," says art department manager Chris Hennah. "New York was one of those sets that seemed like it was simple, but really was quite tricky. We had a far bigger set-dressing department than we had on *The Lord of the Rings* because there were so many shops and all the stuff in the shops had to be purchased.

"You'd go out there and it was just bustling with people," she recalls. "There was a lot of stress, because we had a very tight time frame, but there was a really good spirit. Everybody was helping each other, working with each other—[it was] pretty cool to be a part of."

The switch from Times Square, the showbiz part of town, to Herald Square, a department-store area, happened over a weekend, but some parts of the set were transformed overnight. "We built sets in front of other sets so that we could take them away halfway through shooting to reveal the sets underneath," says Grant. "And we had various prefabri-

The Lyric Vaudeville Theater redressed as the Capitol Theater for a later scene.

cated additions that we could put on to change things as well."

The Alhambra Theater had its canopy craned off to turn it into the Marbridge Building. The automat café in Times Square was a clipped-on facade with Macy's shop frontage behind it, preset with Christmas-themed window displays. The facades could be removed overnight, and a quick switch of canopies completed the transformation.

Many shops just had a change of signs and window dressing to convert them from, say, a drapery to a menswear shop. Some buildings had a quick re-paint and elements such as the door repositioned.

One restaurant was simply boarded over "It was on a corner that, as it transpired, we saw more of than we expected to," says Dan. "So we turned it into a derelict shop that had been boarded up. It happened a lot in those times. That was always our fallback: if it doesn't work, board it up. But we only did it once!"

Peter and crew spent just three weeks filming on the New York set, mostly at night, along with five hundred extras who were hired to populate the city streets.

"The set was great and the extras were really cool," says Carolynne Cunningham, first assistant director. "They were chosen really well, they were just

Peter Jackson gives direction during a night shoot.

good people. It's a thankless job and they were great-spirited and they did everything that was asked of them. It's pretty tough to be asked to go out there every night for a couple of weeks and do a lot of waiting around, and then do something for a little while, and then do a lot more waiting around. They were really good about it."

Filming is a notoriously slow process. In the drive to get everything just right, each shot takes an age to set up, and take after take to film. On *King Kong*, each shot was covered by three different cameras, which added to the setup time since the action, lighting, and background had to be just right from the point of view of all three cameras.

"Some of the shots are so big and complicated, you'd be mad not to cover it from as many angles as you can," says Carolynne. "It also gives Peter and Fran more choices in the cutting room."

The extras each played several different roles. One day they might be angry protesters, one night they might be fleeing from Kong in shock and terror.

Kong will, of course, be added later by the digital effects team at Weta Digital. "We didn't have a twenty-five-foot gorilla rampaging down the street," says Carolynne. "All his interaction, crashing into buildings, and things coming off and things being damaged, it's all going to be digital. All we could do was shoot the surrounding plates, which was the action that goes on around Kong while he's doing that. You can use previz as the tool to see where he's going to be, what he's going to do, and then shoot many people running around the streets in fear, and Jack in his car chasing him."

Adrien Brody, who plays Jack Driscoll, got to do some of his own stunt driving around the streets of the New York set. "I got to drive a thirties cab like a maniac through those streets, which was really, really exciting," says Adrien.

Adrien is an accomplished driver. His training ground for fast driving was the streets of real New York. He grew up there and spent much of his spare time fixing up muscle cars and drag racing. Even so, it is highly unusual for an actor to do his own stunt driving on a movie. Typically a stunt double would stand in for the actor to do such scenes.

"Pete took a gamble with me that day," says Adrien. "He basically mounted four cameras on the car and put me in it—and me driving away from Kong and essentially doing every stunt that I knew, which was reverse 180s and 360s and the e-brakes, slides, and then narrowly missing extras and cars and elevated train tracks, and jumping the curb. It was so exciting."

"He did it really well," says Carolynne. "He didn't do the really, really dangerous stuff—actually hitting the fruit stand and taking the corners very fast when there's stunt people and extras on the streets. That kind of thing we did with Tony Marsh, Adrien's stunt double."

Adrien thinks that the close-ups on Jack driving will look all the more convincing for having been done for real. "You can't fake it," he says. "You have the lights reflecting off the window and you have the vibration of the whole vehicle and the camera shaking and shuddering. And I was nervous, so it was exciting to use that nervous energy to really amp it up. If I had made a mistake, everybody would have gone home early because I had every camera on the car." He laughs. "That's probably one of the most fun days I've had on any movie. All those years of driving around New York paid off."

Full-size exterior *Venture* set on the backlot at Stone Street Studios.

The S.S. *Venture* is tied up at Miramar Wharf, not far from Wellington Airport. It looks like a nineteenth-century tramp steamer, but underneath its grungy, rust-bucket exterior is the *Manuia*, a Dutch fishing boat and trader, built in the 1950s.

"I'd been hunting around for a ship, phoning everyone I knew in various ports around the country," says Dan Hennah, supervising art director. "I was asking about any ships that might look like the one in the original *King Kong*. I'd seen the *Manuia* fifteen years ago and thought, 'Wow, that's a particular type of freighter that just doesn't exist anymore.' I spoke to a friend in Tauranga, who said, 'I'm driving past it right now—it's tied up at the wharf.' I flew up, went on board, and had a look, and the owner was ready to sell. So we got lucky.

"It had just come in from fishing up off Tonga in the central Pacific, and it had forty tons of frozen tuna on board, but couldn't unload in New Zealand because of regulations about where it had caught the fish. But when the owner was able to prove that he'd sold it out of the fishing industry, the New Zealand government let him off-load into containers and transship his fish. So we got it without the fish, thank goodness."

"It needed radical changing," says production designer Grant Major. "The movie is set in 1933, and the *Venture* is an old boat by then—manufactured perhaps sometime around the late 1800s. Back then, it would have had a vertical bow . . . but the *Manuia* had a curved bow. One of the first things we wanted to get right was its silhouette. So we managed to straighten up the bow by this spectacular piece of steelwork that was done with the boat still in the water."

"We ballasted it," Dan explains. "We took water ballast out of the forward end and put [it] down the stern, to ballast the bow up out of the water. We welded on our new bow— just added a piece over the top and then filled it up with ballast again."

The upper decks also had a makeover. "The *Manuia* has the bridge at the back, and the front has a longer cargo-hold area," says Grant. "We wanted the *Venture* to be a multipurpose boat, with a cargo hold as well as being a passenger transport." The original bridge was transformed into Denham's cabin, and more cabins and a wheelhouse were added in front of it.

The layout of the ship was inspired more by the script than by any real-world ship design. "It had to have a bridge, the captain's cabin, Ann's cabin, and Bruce's cabin. It had to have connecting corridors inside and a mess, and it had to have the top deck areas where various dialogue

MARITIME MAKEOVER

Jack Driscoll's "tiger cage" sleeping quarters.

The *Venture*'s hold interior with animal cages.

scenes would happen," says Grant. "So it was a jigsaw puzzle of all these individual scripted pieces, built into a ship."

The script dictated some aesthetic touches as well. "The invented history of the *Venture*," says Grant, "is that Englehorn uses it as a boat for importing animals into New York, hence it's full of cages—on top decks and belowdecks. It gives weight to the fact that the boat is geared up for transporting Kong back to New York, perhaps. And because Jack [Driscoll] wasn't scheduled to be part of the crew, he's living in the tiger's cage, down in the hold.

"There's a humorous aspect to that, but I see an

Between shots on the exterior *Venture* set.

animal cruelty thing to it as well. There was a big importation of animals from around the world back then—they just snatched them out of the jungles and put them in zoos. . . . So there's this thing about animals in cages and the feelings that those images conjure up."

Despite all of this work on the ship itself, most of the scenes set on the *Venture* were not in fact filmed on the *Manuia*. The ship's interiors were all built as individual sets at Stone Street Studios, and another *Venture* set was built on the back lot, surrounded on three sides by blue screen to facilitate special effects shots. And all the sets had to have a specific look.

"It had to look like an old dunger of a boat," says set finishing supervisor Kathryn Lim, whose team had the task of weathering the *Manuia* and the back-lot *Venture* exteriors. "It had to look like it was painted steel with layers and layers of peeling paint,

like the paint has come off but they've not tried to tidy it up, the next year they've just painted over it again. We plastered it to give it a pitty profile, and then we painted. It's really only one layer of paint, but it's been thickened with an acrylic thickener. The rust we created with oxide powders and shellac, or a regular acrylic stain, strategically placed. It gives the feeling it's been here for ages, that the water's seeped up, it's leaching minerals, and it's really gross."

The back-lot boat and many of the studio sets were built on a huge, hinged steel frame so that they could be tilted as needed to simulate movement at sea. "If you shoot ship sets on a gimbal, which lets you move the ship, after about half an hour everyone gets seasick," says Dan. "You get a much more effective ship-at-sea movement in-camera, using little tricks to swing the lights and tilt the water in the jug.

Peter Jackson pauses on the railing of the upper deck, while on the lower deck,
Kyle Chandler receives last-minute makeup and costume touch-ups.

In addition to that, you can tilt the set. It's still stationary, but it has a tilt on the floor, so people have to walk uphill one way and downhill the other way. That helps the illusion that the ship is heeling over, or it's hard up on a rock. You're much better off to trick it than to try and do it for real!"

Once filming on the back-lot *Venture* was completed, the set was dismantled. "We put the very stern of the vessel in the studio with the interior sets, so that you could have the doors open and look out from the galley, along the corridor, and out over the stern," says Dan. "The wheelhouse and the forward cabins went onto the *Manuia*." Part of the dock set was set up beside the *Manuia* at Miramar Wharf, for shots of the *Venture* moving away from the wharf in New York.

Once its filming days are done, what will become of the *Manuia*? "There are all sorts of wonderful ideas for what you could do with it," says Dan. "One of them would be to set the *Venture* up as a museum piece, as a piece of film history, in the shallow water at Greta Point here in Wellington. It's a perfect spot for it."

Adrien Brody with director of photography Andrew Lesnie on the *Venture* set.

Venture exterior set on Stone Street Studios' backlot, with a view of Miramar Heights above the blue screen.

VENTURE
SURABAYA

Skull Island ancient architecture concept design by Gus Hunter.

"Skull Island once had a very rich cultural and extravagant populace, on a par with, say, ancient Peruvian culture. The island was a very successful and beautiful trading port. It had a promenade that ran from the main gate down to the sea. There the people traded with the outer islands.

"They had built in a very rich, Indonesian-influenced style. They mined basalt logs—big, hexagonal stems of crystalline rock—from the coastline of the island and utilized those to tie into the architecture of piled rocks. Almost like you can build a twig house, they were able to strap them and tie them together. That gave them the ability unlike other cultures, to create an ornamental, upswept architectural style to their walls. So their architecture grew to a massive size, because the island had this natural resource. And it grew as a very sophisticated, almost biblical-scale environment.

"The island existed in extreme harmony with its surroundings. The culture of the people had grown up with the knowledge that the island possessed giant gorillas, giant dinosaurs, and an amazing rich and deadly fauna and flora. But they held it at bay with a massive wall that they built around their city, and so controlled their environment. The creatures lived in harmony outside of the wall, the people lived in harmony inside the wall, and everything was in equilibrium.

"But, maybe two thousand years before we enter the story, the seismic eruptions began. Earthquakes began to drop the wall. Slices of the island began to fall away. In fact, the whole island began to sink. That created social chaos within the infrastructure of the city. But also, the wall began to crumble, allowing the creatures into the inner sanctum of the village. Chaos reigned and the people were wiped out. Whether there was infighting, starvation, or they were killed off by these huge predators, we have no idea, but that's ultimately what happened.

"Our natives arrived maybe four generations before we do in 1933 and found the remains of this culture. By now the whole island was distressed and collapsed. Most of the island had sunk. Most of the wall, indeed most of this beautiful island, had gone. The creatures hadn't fallen into the ocean, of course. They had just condensed and moved in. There was one last remaining tiny piece of wall.

"The natives, haplessly blown off course by the winds of the Indonesian oceans, have landed on this desolate, windblown, sea-salt-swept outcrop of

A BRIEF HISTORY OF SKULL ISLAND

AS TOLD BY RICHARD TAYLOR

48

Top: Wide concept by Gus Hunter of the village and fiery wall during Ann's sacrifice to Kong.
Bottom: Concept art by Gus Hunter depicting *Venture* crewmen rowing through a maze of eroded,
ghoulish pinnacle structures as they approach Skull Island.

rock, outside the wall, and there they have to live. There they have to survive. All of their previous culture, the harmony that they had in their previous life and the sophistication of their seafaring, is stripped away, due to basic survival instinct. Their weapons pay no homage to their ancient culture—they're utilitarian, for fishing, hunting, and survival. At best they can fish or hunt seabirds. Beyond the wall, it's rich, lush, full of beautiful food sources, but it's dangerous. Over the wall are the creatures that hold them at bay. So their whole life they stay clinging to this tiny outcrop of rock. Their sole purpose is survival.

"They have no ceremony about them, other than their sacrificial offering to Kong. Every six or twelve months they're sacrificing yet another young woman to appease him, and the gene pool is further deteriorating, causing more and more aggression in the males, because there are less and less women. The feudal system within the culture of the village is so dramatic and so aggressive that they are slowly depopulating and undermining their own survival. They're barely clinging to existence. If we had arrived on the island another sixty years [after] 1933, there's a bloody good chance that they would have died out.

"Our sailors arrive on the island through an underground cave—or so they think. It is actually a massive amphitheater, carved into the solid rock with burial chambers for the gentry of the ancient city. The chamber has split in half and sunk into the ocean. The stairs to the burial chambers are now on a tilt. As the sailors climb up to the point where they pop out in front of the wall, they're actually walking through the old crypts that have been long since stripped of any of their corpses, because the natives, in desperate need of habitation, have pulled the corpses out and now live in the crypts themselves, in amongst the remnants of these ancient people.

"What the sailors discover when they venture across the wall is a saturated ecosystem of creatures. Everywhere you look there are lizards, insects, snails, deadly plants . . . dinosaurs, swamp creatures, and bats. It's all condensed down into this ecosystem unlike anywhere else in the world.

"The city is now totally grown over with dense jungle. But still coming through that are massive architectural structures. The brontosaurs stampede down the boulevard of a massive central city promenade. Eventually, the last remnant of wall is going to fall into the ocean. And, ultimately, what now remains of the island will go with it."

A wide shot of the wall set, representing the bottom third of the wall. The upper two-thirds was built in miniature.

Skull Island is somewhere off the coast of Sumatra, where tectonic plates collide. It is a dangerous place. Its dense jungle is teeming with poisonous things, sharp things, things that bite. Its brutal landscape, forged by violent volcanic eruptions, has been shattered by earthquakes. The island is breaking apart.

An aggressive landscape required the building of aggressive sets, says supervising art director Dan Hennah. "Everywhere you look, you'd expect to see great fissures and cracks, an undercut cliff or a piece of flat land tilted over, a bit of road angling off towards a cliff edge—vertigo-inducing stuff. We're all the time trying to say that the reason no one's found this island is that maybe the whole thing has sunk into the sea. Back in 1933 it was on the way, but maybe now it's gone."

The great wall that once surrounded an ancient city is one of the first indicators of the destructive forces at work on Skull Island. Broken segments of wall tilting into the sea were built as miniatures by Weta Workshop. The art department, meanwhile, built the native village and an enormous section of the wall, including the gates to the overgrown city, on Mount Crawford, just ten minutes' drive from Stone Street Studios.

Although not as large as the New York set, the wall and village set was a huge un-dertaking, constructed over two acres. The set was designed to establish two layers of culture—the flimsy bamboo culture of the current inhabitants and the monumental legacy of an extinct civilization. A dramatic landscape of rock and fissures was roughed out in wooden geometric shapes by the construction department, then clad with polystyrene and concrete. Only the bottom third of the wall was built as a set, with the upper two-thirds being built in miniature. Even so, the wall stood twelve meters high (almost forty feet).

BIG ROCKS AND TREES

"It was a brilliant set—that huge wall was just astounding," says actor Jed Brophy. "When you were going through those huge gates, it wasn't hard to manufacture the feeling of awe and fear because it *was* awesome."

The very top of the wall above the gates was built as a separate set in Studio X. It was seven meters high and included a wall-top walkway and part of the contraption used to sacrifice Ann to Kong. Another set, four meters high, consisted simply of poles on which the native drummers perched high above the wall. The altar, where Kong snatches Ann, was built as a separate set again in Studio Q.

Steve Ingram's special effects team created wind, smoke, and fire for the wall-top scenes. "At the top of the wall we had some in situ propane flames," he says. "We

Top: Interior set of the sacrificial altar. Below: An interior jungle set.

Top: An example of Skull Island architecture. Below: Drystone walling built from spray foam and polystyrene.

had the ability to make them fairly huge, but they wanted the villagers all around the wall—enough in the shot that you couldn't have the flames turned up too high because they were too hot and too close. The natives light some burning liquid, the liquid flows down troughs, then it cuts to the big wall shot with the skull all in flames. In the wide shot it's all digital, but with the natives in the close shots and midshots, that's all real. We made up a mix that was flammable, but not too volatile, that we could pump out of pressure pots. They could light it, then we'd slowly bring the pressure up to create these flowing rivers of flame."

The bridge contraption that delivers Ann to the sacrificial altar was built in two parts: the top part on rollers to initiate the move away from the wall, and a more complete rig to bring her down onto the altar. "It looks like a bamboo structure, but inside it's steel," says construction supervisor Ed Mulholland. "If you're hanging a million-dollar actor off it, it's got to be secure and safe. The closer you get to the actors, the safer things have to be."

Another impressive set was a section of stone pathway and wall, part of the gorge where Denham

and the crew are trampled by a herd of Brontosaurs. It was built at Windy Point on the south coast where there was enough room for the actors to build up some speed to run at full tilt and imagine being chased by dinosaurs. "Peter said, 'You look up to the left and there's a foot, and you look to the right and there's a foot,' so he gave us a pretty good map to where feet were coming down so we were all looking in the right place," says Jed Brophy. "But it took a few takes to get it. It was just a matter of getting in your head that you are terrified and that you're running for your life, but also being able to run and turn around and look at whatever's coming behind you without falling flat on your face. We were running down big stone steps, and that was pretty tricky, because if you missed your footing . . . Someone did fall over at one stage."

For the sculpture department, tasked with fabricating all the rocklike surfaces for the Skull Island sets, the Mount Crawford and Windy Point sets were quite an achievement, according to sculpture supervisor Ra Vincent. Ra's team, numbering sometimes as many as forty carvers, spent months making rock, including the boulders and paving

Simon Harper, 2nd unit on-set art director, setting up Carl Denham's Bell & Howell camera prop at the Brontosaur stampede set.

Bottom of the log chasm's interior studio set, dressed with dinosaur bones.

stones that make up walls, doorways, and roads, the great carved-face statues, and the rocky texture of the jagged landscape. "The wall was a massive build, but the village in front of it was just as massive," he says.

Skull Island's lost civilization built a gigantic dry stone wall anchored by huge columns of natural basalt. Ra's team fashioned boulders and basalt out of spray foam and polystyrene. For the drystone walling, they made thirty-eight panels of boulders, four meters wide and two and a half meters high, with twenty to twenty-five rocks per panel. The panels were then lifted by crane and fixed to scaffolding towers. "Once all the rock panels were on, the scaffolders put up a good working platform all the way around, and we all got up there in our harnesses and made little individual rocks to put in between all the seams."

Polystyrene was also used to texture the landscape in front of the wall. The carvers used chain saws, hot wires, heat guns, angle-grinders, and knives. "Angle-grinding polystyrene, that's one of my favorites," says Ra, "but the Tajima, the biggest snap-blade knife you can buy, is our number one tool. All

our edges had to be supercrisp—nice hard edges, glassy, basalt, lava. They wanted a hard volcanic look, so everything was pointy and nasty. A technique we used . . . for sculpting rocks was to do slight scalloped cuts, which meant that all the high points on your stones had a very sharp edge."

Surfaces intended for heavy foot traffic were strengthened with a layer of concrete, and industrial tinfoil, scrunched up and pressed into the wet cement, gave the concrete a rocky texture. The carvers also used latex molds. Says Ra, "When you wanted a really nice piece, you put a mold of a real rock into the wet cement. Quite often, the following day we'd come back with small barrow loads of cement and make special little bits, because, in the fervor and mayhem of emptying tons and tons of concrete, you can't get too artistic."

To safeguard the actors and stunt performers in action areas, softer rock surfaces were made from rubber sprayed into the molds of real rock. Selected rock faces on Wellington's craggy shoreline were replicated and used many times over. The sculptors scouted for rock faces with just the right qualities. "There was one in Breaker Bay right out on the end of the point," says Ra. "The mold-maker had to walk four hundred meters down the beach with huge pails of silicone and generators and heaters and spend a couple of days out there taking texture stamps off the natural rock walls."

Once sculpted, the rock surfaces were plastered and painted by the set finishers, and the greens department added lichens, gravel, and grit. Set dressers scattered broken shells and burnt wood, erected the bamboo structures of the latter-day natives, and decorated the set with skulls and corpses.

The gruesome job of making and mangling human remains for the set fell to Weta Workshop. About forty generic body shapes were cast in urethane from two different molds, then chopped and

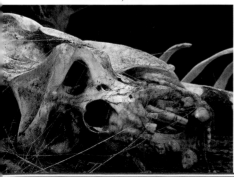

Life-size skull of Kong's father.

changed for individualized looks, says workshop supervisor Jason Docherty: "You just cut the head off, turn the head, cut the arm off, change the orientation of the arm, and put latex and tissue all over it to give it this mummified look."

Weta Workshop also provided skeletons, skulls, and bones for other Skull Island sets, including a hundred bodies' worth of human bones for the bone fields where the remains of Kong's past sacrificial victims lie. "They're cheap plastic skeletons," reveals Jason. "A human body has two hundred and something bones, so to mold a human skeleton costs thousands of dollars. You can buy full Halloween skeletons, unassembled, from a commercial company in America that has them made in China and they're only one hundred dollars each. We dolled them all up. We just did it one weekend. In some cases we made them look like they've got a little bit of meat on them, and then we painted them up for the bone fields."

Weta Workshop also made jumbo-size bones for Kong's lair, a studio set. They represent the skeleton of Kong's father or mother, suggesting he once had a family and has not always been a solitary creature. The props makers stuck hair and latex to the bones to make it look as though the animal's fur is still rotting away.

The set dressers decorated that part of the lair with spiderwebs made from "some horrible toxic stuff that they put into padded bras," says Tanea Chapman, supervising set dresser. "You heat it up to a really hot temperature and put it in a cobweb-spinning gun on the end of a drill. It spits out in a circle and laces itself and looks like a spiderweb. You can stretch it and you can wrap things in it. It's fantastic."

Most of the jungle sets were built in New Zealand's largest soundstage, the brand-new Kong Stage, constructed at Stone Street Studios just in time for filming. In fact, the roof was going onto the soundstage as the set for the killing ground, where

Kong disposes of his victims, was being built inside. The Stone Street Studios complex was once a gasworks and later a paint factory, so many of the studios and workshops are converted warehouses. Kong Stage is a purpose-built soundstage, 24,500 square feet in area and forty feet high—room for plenty of trees, rocks, and big background blue screens.

The art department was undaunted by the prospect of building a jungle, having developed considerable expertise on *The Lord of the Rings*. "We'd worked on Fangorn Forest and established a whole lot of techniques for building forests," says Dan Hennah. "A jungle's got a lot of very similar elements—big trees, lots of foliage." The brief for Skull Island was to create a fantastical yet realistic-looking jungle, so the sets include both real and man-made plants and trees.

Out back, behind the stages, the art department built four greenhouses and a couple of shade houses for a jungle style nursery. They spent six months researching jungle flora and shopping for plants in forests, nurseries, and farms throughout New Zealand, then filled the greenhouses with live tree ferns, climbers, grasses, mosses, and all manner of slightly unusual plants.

With Jack Driscoll, Carl Denham, and the sailors trekking all through the jungle in search of Ann, many different jungle sets were required. The greens team, at times as many as fifty people, has been kept frantically busy rearranging greenery. "They film for a couple of days, or a day," says greens foreman Simon Lowe, "and then we have a night shift come in and completely change the set to a swamp, or remove foliage, or just try and change the look. So the sets are constantly revolving and changing, which is great for the film crew, but very taxing for us."

Top: Vines made out of soft rubber. Below: Production designer Grant Major directing construction at the Skull Island swamp set on the backlot at Stone Street Studios.

Taxing for the greenery too—studio lighting takes its toll on live foliage. The greens team lavishes care and attention on the plants, keeping them constantly damp, sending them back to the nursery when they start to droop, and replenishing the sets with fresh foliage every couple of days. But after two or three stints on set, plants such as mosses start to look a bit sad, says Simon. "So then we can break them up and use them as forest litter on the forest floor or in ruts and dark places where you have a lot of organic matter building up."

Nestled among the live flora on the jungle sets is a huge variety of artificial plants, from big trees to small lichens. "If you have a big studio like Kong Stage, trying to fill that with real greens would be an ecological disaster. To have a balance of artificial and real is the key. If you have it all artificial, it really stands out, but if you have a few real elements amongst it, it sells it." For example, moss seen in the foreground of a shot is likely to be real, bought from moss farms; in the background, a carpet of moss-colored, slightly singed fake fur looks indistinguishable from the live moss.

Two containerloads of artificial plants and flowers were shipped in from China, but many plants have been made on-site by the art department. A special prehistoric department was set up to develop the more oddball flowers and plants, says Dan Hennah. "We've had three to five people working for almost a year, making upside-down flowers and insect-eating plants, largely based on historical research into now extinct plants from the dinosaur era, but also some slightly fanciful variations—great big spongy, slippery flowers."

Overhead shot of the swamp set.

Vines can be made out of foam: "Just like your bed-mattress foam, but in cords, just dipped through latex baths," says Simon. "We also burnt and textured a lot of rope, trying to add some interest to it—you get a bit of a gnarly effect with it. We made up a series of sections of vines using a mold, and that worked quite well for the larger vines. They're a soft rubber and they have a texture of pohutukawa bark on them. And we've used a lot of native supplejack as well."

And then there are the big trees—as many as fifty or sixty for one piece of jungle. They needed to be lightweight, easy to maneuver, premade, and ready to be swung into position at a moment's notice. Glancing around the Stone Street Studios lot, one might be forgiven for thinking someone has run amok with a chain saw. The fences and exterior walls are lined with fallen tree trunks. Closer in-spection reveals that they are made of polystyrene.

"If the tree is not too complicated with shapes and sizes, we use polystyrene," says Simon. "If we start getting a lot of limbs and laterals and a lot of weight on them, we build a steel structure and clad it in polystyrene. You've got to get the engineering and counterbalancing right before you start cladding."

Building a single tree involves several different teams within the art department. The engineers build the steel armature; the carvers sculpt the polystyrene; the mold-maker makes molds of real bark; the set fin-ishers plaster over the polystyrene, use the molds to stamp an imprint of bark texture into the plaster, then paint the tree; the greens team dresses it with leaves and vines. For more detailed bark textures, many tree trunks are wrapped in rubber bark, from molds taken off macrocarpa or pohutukawa trees. Taller trees tend

Peter Jackson walks along Skull Island's rocky shore.

Climbing among fake trees on an interior jungle set.

not to require a canopy of leaves. Their trunks end abruptly as if the upper trunk and branches have been sawn off, and the foliage will be created by Weta Digital. Those that do require leaves have the tips of real branches grafted onto them and sprays of plastic and silk foliage attached by hand. "One tree might end up with twelve thousand sprays on it, depending on the size of the tree," says Simon, "and they're all individually put on."

The hollow log in which Ann seeks refuge from some hungry carnivores was ten meters (almost thirty-three feet) long and two meters (six and a half feet) in diameter. The biggest upright trees were six meters (nineteen and a half feet) high and about ten meters in diameter at ground level. "They were rising up out of the water of the swamp," says Dan. "In terms of the degree of difficulty, they were the hard-est. They had to be light enough for us to move around, but not so light that they floated in the swamp. So they've got concrete in the bottom, not too much foam."

A swamp was created outside on a patch of parking lot doubling as a back lot at Stone Street Studios. A rim for the wet set was built up using wire baskets packed with rocks, and the set was then filled with 1.8 million liters (nearly five hundred thousand gallons) of water. The set finishers colored the water with food dye and made pond scum to float on the surface. "We used beaded polystyrene just ground off a polystyrene block," says set finishing supervisor Kathryn Lim, "and we colored that in a concrete mixer with paint and then, when it was dry, chucked it in the pool."

Coming up with recipes for such unlikely items as pond scum typically involves expertise, trial and error, and sometimes a little bit of serendipity. Wax beads and bean-bag balls were used for earlier attempts at making pond scum, but they looked too symmetrical. Grinding the polystyrene produced beads of different sizes. "When you broke down the beads, there was this kind of weird, kinetic, magnetic thing going on with the scum, so they clung to each other. So, when the boat went through the water, the pond scum parted and then it closed in again behind. It turned out really well."

A patch of Skull Island's rocky shore was also built as a wet set. The greens team obtained consent to collect seaweed washed up around Wellington's coastlines for the set. Set dressers scattered seashells and glued fake limpets to the rocks. "The props makers made these lovely little anemones, and the guys glued them just under the waterline before they filled the water up," says supervising set dresser Tanea Chapman. "When you looked in rock pools, you saw these little jellied anemones." Not that audiences are likely to look that close; "You'll never see any of it," she says with a rueful laugh.

Even mud has been specially made for the Skull Island sets. Typical ingredients for hygienic, colorfast mud are sterilized peat and wallpaper paste. A ready supply of waste sawdust from the construction department provides the raw material for a variety of other set finishings. "We've spent hours and hours on sawdust . . . because they'd want tiny little bits of dirt and larger pieces of peat and things like that," says Kathryn. "We'll mix sawdust, plaster, and paint and just throw it at the set. It just splats on and looks like moss or lichen."

In one of the most memorable scenes from the 1933 version of *King Kong*, Kong shakes the *Venture* search party off a huge log spanning a deep ravine. The sequence was an extraordinary special effects achievement for its time, combining the stop-motion Kong puppet and a miniature tree trunk with footage of the actors walking up and falling off an unseen ramp. In Peter Jackson's *King Kong*, the actors were able to fall off the log itself, but the log was built in three separate pieces.

The log chasm set, in Kong Stage, consisted of the two opposite edges of the chasm, but not the chasm itself, which would be built as a miniature. Each side of the chasm sported one end of the log—a fallen tree—with the middle of the log missing. The chasm on set was just one meter deep on one side and two meters on the other, so the actors were able to emerge from the jungle, walk along the edge of the ravine, and step onto the log on one side of the set, and later step off the log on the other side of the set.

All the action on the fallen trunk was filmed in Stage A against blue screens. The missing middle section of the trunk was built on a computer-controlled motion rig so its movement could be programmed to match the actions of the digital Kong. The log was made of polystyrene with a steel frame running through it, soft rubber bark, and safety mats on the floor beneath it. Anchor points were built into the log so that the actors and stunt performers could be harnessed to it if necessary. For the most violent movements, stuntmen stood in for the actors. The actors were swapped in for close-ups of their characters clinging to the bucking log for dear life.

The log marked the end of the road for Jed Brophy's character, Skeggs, who survived such dangers as the swamp and the Brontosaur stampede only to plunge to a sticky fate at the log chasm. "I died a very innocuous death when I just fell to my death in the pit. I would have loved it to have been a bit more gruesome." Jed laughs. "The log was a big hydraulic thing and it lifted up and down and we just fell off it onto a mat. And that was the end of me as far as I know. Once I'm dead, I get eaten by a giant slug, I'm told, but I haven't seen the slug, so I couldn't tell you."

61

Clockwise: Greg Broadmore creature concept for V-Rex. Christian Pearce creature concept for V-Rex. Greg Broadmore concept for V-Rex.

Only one creature design from the 1996 preproduction phase has made it into the 2005 version of *King Kong:* the brontosaur.

"Pretty much everything else was designed from scratch," says Weta Workshop concept designer Greg Broadmore. "We did hundreds and hundreds of drawings and sculpts. And there were dozens more for all the creatures that didn't make it into the film as well."

The team took a scattergun approach, putting every idea down on paper, no matter how weird or wacky. They worked independently, dashing off rough pencil sketches, then scanning the drawings into their computers and coloring them in Photoshop.

"We were concentrating on not doing what the other guy was doing at first," says conceptual designer Christian Pearce, "rather than trying to get cohesive before we put anything in front of Peter."

"I probably did twenty or thirty different V-Rex designs," says Greg. "To start with, I wanted to just draw the coolest V-Rex I could think of."

"Greg and I were big dinosaur fans before *King Kong,* big fans of *Jurassic Park,*" says Christian. "But we didn't want our rex looking like the *Jurassic Park* rex."

Peter Jackson's responses to their first illustrations gave the designers a clear sense of directions to explore. He liked one drawing of a V-Rex with rotten meat hanging out of its teeth and another with its eye poked out.

"We quickly realized that Peter wanted the most evil, diabolical, monstrous V-Rex you could imagine," says Greg. "It wasn't about making it a real dinosaur. It was about making it the most terrifying thing that Kong could fight. We worked on making the eyes scary, and making it nasty and smelly—which is a recurring theme in this movie!" He laughs.

"There was talk early on of the rex being a lot more upright, like in Charles Knight's old paintings, where it used to walk around like a man with his tail dragging along the ground," says Christian.

"Charles Knight was a famous dinosaur artist, one of the original dinosaur artists who still influences today," says Greg. "A lot of his old dinosaurs were crocodilian, reptilian, and had traits that aren't represented in dinosaurs anymore. The modern scientific dinosaur has very fine scales, but Pete wanted it to be more archaic, so I asked if he wanted the crocodile scales. To put crocodile scales on a dinosaur is kind of ludicrous, but it makes it look cooler and gives it an older-fashioned Ray Harryhausenesque look."

The decision to go with a crocodilian

THE CREATURES

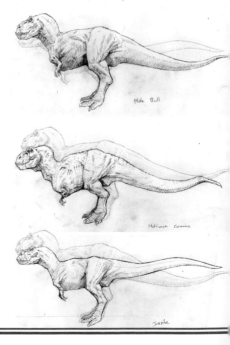

Greg Broadmore creature concept for V-Rex.

another one turns up and it's gnarlier and scarier than the last one. And finally the third one turns up and it's the biggest of all. We wanted them not just to be bigger and nastier, but to have their own individual qualities.

"We thought of them as this group of ornery yokels, this inbred family of dinosaurs—the matriarch, the bull, and the juvenile. We really wanted the matriarch to be this beaten-up, old, grizzled character. Everything about her is a bit more withered and sunken in than the others. She's starting to sag. Her torso and tail are hanging lower than her hips. The bull is heavily muscled and has this big butting kind of heavy-boned head. And the juvenile is slimmer,

Greg Broadmore size comparison of V-Rex bull, matriarch, and male juvenile.

skin texture cost the production hundreds of man-hours. "They were such a time-consuming thing to sculpt," reveals Christian. "But it was a great defining characteristic which really separates it from the *Jurassic Park* rex—that heavy scaling running down its back."

The designers played around with scarring to give the V-Rexes a battle-hardened look. One V-Rex was drawn with a raking of scars across its muzzle, which Greg figures could have been picked up in a fight or perhaps during eating. "I'd imagine that it had just pulled its head out of a rib cage," he says. "The way it feeds, it would just jam its head into another dead creature and get out what it could, but as it's going through all the bones, it's damaging itself. V-Rexes don't care about those little injuries. It's just a skin wound for a V-Rex.

"We were always trying to rationalize everything," Greg says, laughing, "definitely trying to ground it in reality, because as crazy as you go with your design, at the end of the day you've got to pull it back to something that works.

"Peter wanted the V-Rexes to be three different characters," Greg says. "You see one V-Rex try to attack Ann, and you think, 'oh my God, it's almost bigger than Kong.' And then suddenly, what the hell, more graceful, more poised, and he has a more classic dinosaur posture where he's very horizontal. There was tons of work in making them individuals."

"None of these are real rexes as we know them, but they have the basic traits of large theropods," says Christian. "My guys were a little more front-heavy than Greg's were. He always seemed to put the weighting of the rex further behind the hips than I did. I always tried to have that forward-heavy aspect to it to give him that lower-down head, which to me looks more aggressive and spookier.

"It was a pretty intense illustrative period, but once it had gotten past the first two passes with Peter, it got taken over by the sculptors, and they did so much of the work themselves. None of the V-Rex drawings show that thin, nimble waist that they ended up with, for instance. So much was resolved in the sculpt."

Ann Darrow and Jack Driscoll escape from Kong's lair with the unlikely aid of a Terapusmordax flying creature. "That was a fun one," says Christian. "You could just try anything you wanted. Warren, another of the conceptual designers, was working from out of town and we'd get a shipment from him every couple of days: 'Oh, my goodness! Look what he was thinking! Let's steal some of those ideas.' And he'd get ours and some of those ideas would trigger things in him too. It was right towards the end of the creature design process. We were all fighting to get our little bits into this guy. I think a bit of all of us ended up in it.

"Infected-looking was what Peter kept mentioning. Right from the start we were talking about naked mole rats, which are hideous-looking little creatures. That was a basis for

Christian Pearce creature concept for V-Rex.

the coloring and the skin texture— that real saggy, baggy, loose skin just kind of dripping off the musculature of the creature. Peter wanted it to have skin diseases and disgusting wetness to it. I had some photos of worms and naked mole rats, and even young Siamese short-haired cats with that same sort of wrinkly hairlessness to them. Batlike wings were another one. It needed to be large enough so that it could almost pick a person up, and basically humanoid shape, Peter said."

Not all of the designs were entirely practical. "There were some where the wings were mounted on its back legs," says Christian, "which caused a bit of an uproar amongst some of the zoologists here, who said that creatures can't fly with their back legs. But we were just putting everything out there, trying new things to see what's going to catch Peter's eye."

"In one of the more preposterous ones I did," says Greg, "I gave it a big, gross belly, which I thought was kind of funny, but it did make it less likely as a flying creature. So it

Terapusmordax flying creature concept by Greg Broadmore.

ended up thin. In the end, on the final scannable maquette, we pushed it even further, made it as emaciated as possible."

Exploring the look of a creature raises questions about its lifestyle, its diet, or where it lives on the island, and the answers all affect the design. "Whenever we talk to Peter, he'll give us little tidbits of what the creature gets up to and what it needs to be able to do," says Christian. "The Terapusmordax flying creature was going to be living up in the mountains, and it seems to be a guy who's quite social—they go out hunting in packs. They've got big, strong feet and sicklelike toes, which they use for hunting and for hanging upside down from the roof like a bat."

"Peter really drove us a long way with the flying creature," says Greg. "He kept on pushing us. In the end he came back with this idea of it having skin like a sphinx cat . . . and we started introducing little sores and making them horrible, scabby little creatures, and that was a great deal of fun.

"You try to think of every trick that makes it disgusting, what grosses you out, and what grosses Peter out. In one drawing I tried to take it to an absolute extreme, as foul as I could make it, in this pile of yellow sludge like it's practically melting—grotesque, all inflamed, with varicose veins under the skin. Then we did rabbit variants, which are much more rodent-

like and doglike, and Pete really liked the taut skin over the rib cage with all the excess skin around the joints, and just how . . . diseased it looked."

Once Peter was happy with the look of the Terapusmordax flying creature's body, the designers sculpted a small design maquette in plasticine and then experimented with different heads for it. "We did probably twenty or thirty sculptures just of the head," says Greg. "We nailed down various characteristics from the different sculpts—the teeth from one and skull of another. And even when we started sculpting the head on the final scannable maquette, there were revisions."

The huge, predatory Piranhadon swamp creature that knocks the sailors off their rafts was based on an early illustration by conceptual artist Gus Hunter. Although Peter liked Gus's concept, he asked the designers to explore variations.

Terapusmordax flying creature scannable maquette.

Terapusmordax flying creature design maquette.

"I was looking at seal anatomy for its fins. It needed quite a strong torso and limbs to support itself on the water," says Christian. "The head was always inspired by those deep-sea angler fish with those long, pointy teeth. And the large eyes are also a low-light deep-sea feature, which probably doesn't make a lot of sense for a swamp-based creature, but he's a cool-looking guy. For all the going around the block that it did, it ended up staying pretty close to Gus's original drawing. Gus almost nailed it right from the get go."

Many of the incidental creatures of Skull Island, such as insects, centipedes, and a Scorpiopede, were quickly designed and quickly approved. "A lot of these drawings, Peter [approved] on the first pass and gave them to the digital guys, who built them straight in the computer. There were no sculpts of them done here," says Christian.

When Kong knocks Ann's would be rescuers off the log spanning a deep chasm, they fall into a pit full of all sorts of vile creatures. The scene in the pit was almost, but not quite, in the original film, says Greg. "In the 1933 *King Kong* when they fall into the pit, as they hit the ground, you kind of see a couple of shapes in spidery forms, and Jack Driscoll fights off a lizardy creature at the end, but you don't really get to see it because it was cut from the film, and unfortunately that footage was lost. But Pete wanted to reinstate it in his version of the film because he thought it was a great terrifying moment. So we got to design lots of creepy, crawly, insecty creatures. I'm really looking forward to the pit sequence. It's really scary. There are probably half a dozen different life-forms down there—mostly crustaceans, but also slugs and spidery things and a giant weta, which is very close to a real weta—it's kind of an überweta."

"We were trying to get crabs in the movie right from the get-go," says Christian. "Peter was only half-interested in them at the start, but a couple of our giant crabs ended up in the pit. We were both big crab fans before we started on this. They're just like little tanks that walk around, little armored dudes with these huge weapons out the front. They're pretty impregnable, and they can do a lot of damage. They seem like ready made Skull Island locals."

Piranhadon swamp creature mouth detail.

Scorpiopede maquette designed and sculpted by Christian Pearce.

Rigid Geo for Kong animation.

Animation director Eric Leighton would crawl inside his computer if he could. He snatches at the little gray representation of Kong currently on his screen: "I want to just get in there and grab that guy and move him around!" He laughs.

Eric, animation director Christian Rivers, and a team of fifty animators are responsible for bringing myriad creatures in *King Kong* to life—"primarily Kong, the star of the show," says Eric, "but it's a Peter Jackson movie, so there are lots and lots of monsters, lots of dinosaurs, lots of action, and we're responsible for the performances on all those guys."

The Kong on Eric's screen is a far cry from the fleshed-out, furry version audiences will see on the big screen. This little Kong is represented by a series of cylinders in shades of gray. "A representation of the volume of everything on the character has been attached to his skeleton," says Eric. "In other words, you take a cylinder that is roughly sculpted into the shape of his upper arm, and you attach it to his upper arm bone. Each of these little slices around his torso is attached to one of the vertebrae on his spine. So when you animate the bones, the bones then drive this 3D representation of bits of his body. But this is just for animation. And the only reason we do this in animation is speed. We can move this guy around very fast."

Animating any version of Kong more complex than this hollow collection of cylinders would be laboriously slow. "You'd have to move his arm a bit and then wait a minute," says Eric. For this reason, the animators are happiest when working with the simplest of puppets. "For all the really good animators that I've worked with, the faster they work, the better the work is, because . . . they're feeling the flow and the motion and the performance."

Despite not being able to physically take hold of the Kong on his screen, Eric considers digital animation to be much like the stop-motion, frame-by-frame animation that Willis O'Brien used for the original *Kong*. The digital puppet can be posed in any position, just as a physical stop-motion character can be posed. "You put a lot of animation controls on the digital puppet, and then you can move it around, just like you can move an armature," Eric says "To animate it, you would position it wherever you want it and basically take a 3D snapshot of that pose, which is called a key frame. Then you'd say, 'One second later I want this arm to be here,' so you'd move it and take a snapshot there. So then, in one second, you'll see it going in a straight line from here to here. But then you say, 'Okay, a half a second in, I want the hand to go here,' and you take another snapshot of that. Now when you scrub through that

ANIMATION

same second, it will actually describe an arc. You end up putting thousands of key frames on every single shot on every joint."

Before the animators launch into the more bone-crunching, tooth-and-claw, action-packed moments in the movie, they take each creature for a quiet stroll. Animation supervisor Atsushi Sato has been testing walk cycles and exploring how creatures might run, swim, fly, or gallop.

"Each character has its own behavior and style of action," he says. "Before we start production shots, we need to define the character—how fast it moves, how big its stride is, what its wing cycle should be. We have many types of characters—insects, bats, also digital doubles that stand in for humans. Animating humans is difficult. People know how they move, so you have to make it quite realistic."

Scale is an especially significant factor in defining the movement style of the larger creatures. "Why do people like dinosaurs? Because they are huge," says Atsushi. "We have to make them look big. But we also want them to be quite active and fast. If we animate the character too fast, it will make it look smaller. We have to find the point that it moves fast but still looks huge."

An impression of enormous weight can be given by having relatively large areas of a creature's body affected by each move. "When a dinosaur turns his head," says Atsushi, "if we move just his head, it looks light. If we make his shoulders follow through as the head turns, that's the thing that makes the character look heavy."

The animators have been working on movement styles for Kong himself for months. "Right now we are changing Kong's concept a little bit," says Atsushi. "He started out more like a monster type, but now we are moving into more naturalistic gorilla-like movement, in terms of facial expression and behavior."

Many hours' worth of documentary footage on

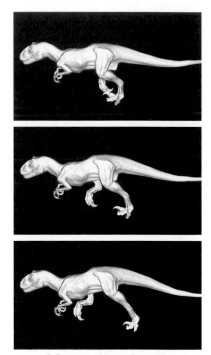

Different stages of the raptor's run cycle.

A raptor motion test.

gorillas has given the animators a wealth of reference material, but not all of Kong's movement styles can be based on the actions and behavior of real gorillas as caught on film. "We have footage of gorillas quite agitated. They threaten, they intimidate others to protect the group, but they don't really fight for life," says Atsushi. "They are kind of hitting each other, but they're just playing."

"It's an exaggerated reality," says Eric, "so we want the power and believability underneath, but then we want to entertain on top. So we're making them all characters—not just Kong but the dinosaurs as well. We're quite a bit more active with using tails as a performance device on the dinosaurs. They're predatory and they . . . start sweeping around and getting excited about stuff," he says, slapping and swishing his arm heavily on the tabletop, "which we wouldn't do on a naturalistic documentary-type film. It is characterizing on top of the reality of what they are.

"There's a lot of fighting in this movie and Kong punches a lot of dinosaurs. That punch, when he hits their head, it takes a long time for that wave of momentum to go all the way through their body to the end of their tail. It's not like human scale where you punch them and they just go down. You punch that dinosaur and . . ." Eric sends a slow, exaggerated wave of motion rippling down his own body, from head to tail-

bone. "Any tricks like that to show scale. It's reality-based. We do want that stuff to feel as real as possible, but they have to play huge. I think everything in this movie is huge. Kong is huge, the dinosaurs are huge, the trees are huge, the rocks are huge, the ferns are huge—everything is huge!" He laughs.

"All that motion then transfers over onto a beastie with skin, and there's a whole muscle system that goes inside of him . . . if I stop like this"—he slams his fist down on the desk—"you see there's a shake on my biceps. Hopefully once the muscle model is working, some of that stuff will be 'automatic.' I don't want to hand-animate that on every muscle—it would be insane, we'd need six years! So we'll automate as much as possible. But if I want to communicate tension by having the tendons standing out in the neck, that's a performance issue and I would have to hand key-frame that. There are lots of little details like that that we need to key-frame."

Most scenes have been roughed out in advance by the previz team, giving the animators a clear guide to what a creature needs to be doing in any given shot. "Previz is . . . visual storytelling, brainstorming, coming up with gags and different ideas," says Eric. "It's working on how the characters interact with each other. All the rough performances and general timing and positioning are worked out at the previz stage. But then we take that and make it bigger on each step of the path."

In fine-tuning a character as complex as Kong, the animators face a multitude of choices and performance issues. "We're playing Kong's performance very animal," says Christian Rivers. "And I don't mean just that he's running around on all fours like a gorilla. As an animal, he's always in the now. An ani-

Animation shows Kong swinging on vines as he fights a V-Rex.

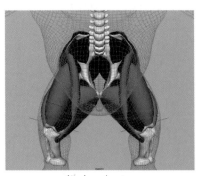

Kong's muscle system.

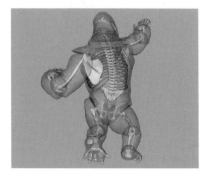

A Kong animation skeleton rig.

mal doesn't really know when it's dying. They know when they're wounded and they react instantaneously to the pain, and they'll carry a limb if it's hurt, but they won't sit there and mope about the fact that they're in pain."

The animators have chosen to pull back from overly expressive facial animation for Kong. "We're trying to make his performance very subtle and keep him very enigmatic," says Christian, who believes that Kong's lack of sentimentality about his situation will allow audience members to respond to him with their own emotions.

"It's something that worked very well in the previz. We chose not to include any facial animation and keep this rather blank character face of Kong. But the Empire State Building sequence where he dies packed a huge emotional punch with everyone who watched it. Kong wasn't investing in his own demise. He was just an animal that was being killed and was trying to protect Ann."

Christian has been working with actor Andy Serkis on the motion capture stage, where Andy is further developing the character aspects of Kong's performance. "Andy's an amazing actor and he's studied gorillas inside out," says Christian. "I talk

about the specifics of the shot as far as the action that Kong needs to be doing, but Andy's totally looking into the motivations and getting under the skin of what Kong is and why he's doing it."

Andy's performances as Kong can be captured on computer and used instead of key-frame animation to drive the digital Kong for many scenes, but not without some tweaking. "The only way to really turn Andy into Kong is to augment his performance. Once it's in the computer you digitally alter his physiology. So certain steps that Andy may take with his legs would need to be made shorter. The amount of weight that he puts on his arms when he comes down on his hands . . . we'd need to add animation into the shoulders. It's basically embellishing it, but still using all Andy's performance choices that he made on the day."

But for many action-packed moments, such as the battle between Kong and the V-Rexes, Kong's animation will most likely be key-framed. "You can get some fantastic results both ways," says Christian. "Where Andy's performance has become invaluable is anything where there's a connection with Ann."

Meanwhile, Eric can sometimes be found on all

fours on the set, helping to ensure that the live action fits in with the digital action in visual effects shots. "I've been lucky enough to get on set quite a bit . . . working with the stunties and actors to tell them where the invisible dinosaurs are and where the invisible giant monkey is and where they need to look. We just did a sequence with Adrien Brody on set which was really fun. To just run around and throw myself on the ground and pretend I'm twenty-five feet tall, slamming my fists in anger and all that, it's a really great experience." Eric laughs. "And often we come up with ideas on set. If you're working with the actors or the stunties, they'll say, 'Oh, that's cool,

but what if I do this as well.' Every step of the way, more excitement and energy gets put into it.

"It's constantly evolving here—lots of creativity at every level," says Eric. "That's the way that Peter Jackson works. It's the best and worst of working for him. The worst part is that you can never be sure of anything. You can bleed on something and love it and love it, and then all of a sudden it's gone. It's hard sometimes to let go, but you know it's always making the movie better. The best part is, Peter really, really fosters creative input from everybody on the crew. And ultimately when you see the final product, you feel a part of yourself in it."

73

Final shot of Kong confronting his foe.

Naomi Watts and Adrien Brody share a dramatic moment.

Kong's lair is an island of broken rock surrounded by floor-to-ceiling blue screens and a clutter of filmmaking paraphernalia. Naomi Watts, as Ann Darrow, lies as if asleep in a nest of padded blue blocks representing Kong's hand. Behind her, a twisted mass of roots, vines, grasses, moss, and dark rock winds its way up to the lighting grid. On a ledge just above her is an immense skull, standing in for Kong's head. It has been borrowed from the skeleton of one of Kong's ancestors—a scattering of enormous ribs, knucklebones, and femurs on another rocky set, for now pushed aside behind the coffee urns and snack table at the far end of the soundstage.

Adrien Brody, as Jack Driscoll, is scheduled to sneak into the lair all day.

"Playback!" orders the first assistant director.

Music fills the warehouse—"Braveheart: Revenge." It has an urgent beat and a tone of energized suspense. The amplified sound of slow, heavy breathing crashes over it, like waves hitting a rocky shore.

"And . . . action!"

Adrien creeps over a tangle of thick roots and straw, shrinks against an outcrop of rock as he skirts past two blue poles representing Kong's outflung arm, and inches toward Naomi. "Ann!" he whispers. "Ann!" She opens her eyes, sees him.

Slowly, slowly, they reach out to each other, fingertips almost touching . . .

"Eyes!" calls director Peter Jackson. Their eyes fly to the skull. The heavy breathing changes to a surprised grunt.

"And up!"

Naomi jolts her body as if suddenly snatched upward. Adrien stumbles back.

"And cut!"

Naomi and Adrien drop out of character. The music and grunts cease. Actor Andy Serkis, the source of Kong's heavy breathing, climbs down from his perch atop an A-frame ladder half-hidden in a forest of fans, tripods, and lighting stands. He fishes a set of false gorilla teeth out of his mouth and settles down to write some notes on a laptop computer.

Three actors are playing this scene, but only two of them can be physically present on the set. Kong will be added by Weta Digital later in postproduction. In a few weeks' time, Andy will start driving the digital Kong's performance through the magic of motion capture. For now, though, he is sidelined. He is simply too small to stand in for the twenty-five-foot gorilla.

"I've been his thumb," he points out.

A crew member walks past with his arm completely encased in a huge blue finger. In the shadows, behind trolleyloads of camera equipment, another crew member is wrapping a pole with foam and blue

ON SET WITH KONG

A crew member holds up Kong's "finger" on set.

fabric. Both digits will be used to prod and thwack Naomi or her stunt double in the days to come.

"We use everything we can think of to give a sense of Kong's presence: sound, height, creating parts of him physically," says Andy. "I've picked Naomi up and walked her and put her down. I've been Kong's fist squeezing her, so she can physically hold on to me and feel like she's being squeezed by Kong's hand. And I'm doing the breathing and his vocalizations."

Enter the Kongalizer, a piece of software magicked up by postproduction sound wizard Chris Ward and hooked up to the set-side sound system. Andy puts in his fake teeth, cups his hands over his mouth, and makes animal noises into a microphone, feeding every breath, growl, and throat rattle to the Kongalizer, which distorts and reverbs the sounds in such a way that, when amplified, they sound like the cavernous vocalizations of an enormous beast. Simply put, Andy's voice goes into the Kongalizer and comes out as the voice of Kong.

"It's a way of evoking Kong spatially, and giving him size," says Andy. More than the giant blue fingers and ancestral skull, his Kongalized voice creates a sense of Kong's presence for the other actors: he is living, he is breathing, he is huge, and he is right here in his lair.

"Sometimes," says Andy, "I'll actually speak

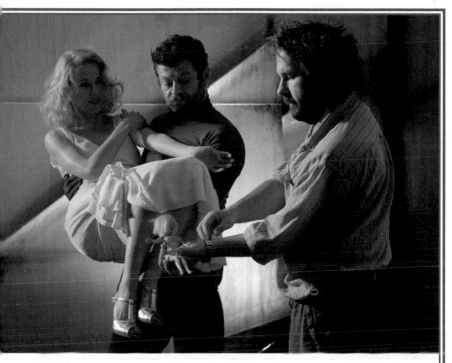

Andy Serkis participated on set in a number of ways, including holding Naomi Watts, to give a sense of Kong's physical presence.

Kong's subtext or physicalize his actions: 'Kong is rising, he's rising up. He's beating his chest . . .' Then the cameras know to lift up too. I'll be emoting as Kong but calling out as myself: 'And now I'm smashing Jack! I'm smashing him with my left fist! And now I'm stomping him! I'm rising up! I'm beating my chest!' That energizes the scene."

Adrien creeps into Kong's lair again, but now the cameras are close on Naomi.

Peter Jackson guesses the *Braveheart* theme isn't working for her: "Do you want some emotional music? 'Reaching for the Moon,' would that work for you?"

Sound recordist Hammond Peek cues up the song from a library of tracks chosen by screenwriters

Fran Walsh and Philippa Boyens: "Mozart," "Al Jolson," "Drumming," and "Hollow Log Music," among others.

"We started playing in music at the green-screen stage," Hammond explains. "A large part of my job is to create atmosphere for the actors. Not much of the sound we record is usable."

That's not because he is bad at his job. The huge fans used to give Skull Island a windswept look make quite a racket. Many of the filming venues are warehouses with thin brick walls, construction sites next door, planes overhead, and rain on their tin roofs. For most scenes, the actors will return during postproduction to rerecord their dialogue. The dialogue

Hammond records on set will primarily serve as a guide track.

"Playback!"

Andy breathes. The smooth voice of Ella Fitzgerald croons out:

The moon and you appear to be
So near and yet so far from me . . .

"Ann! Ann!" Adrien and Naomi reach out to each other. Naomi's eyes fill with tears. The wind whips at her face.

"Cut! That one was a bit blinky," calls Peter from his comfy sofa, where he sits with Fran and Philippa,

watching a set of monitors receiving video feeds from the cameras.

Naomi wipes the tears away. The cameras roll again. She sees Adrien and her eyes mist over. She doesn't blink. She reaches out to him . . . so near and yet so far.

"Eyes! And up! And cut!"

"I loved the way you allowed yourself a slight smile at Jack," Peter says to Naomi.

"Naomi's an actress who's very much used to playing off every moment and receiving what another actor does," notes Andy . . . which is all very well for developing the Ann/Jack romance,

Andy Serkis gives Naomi Watts a focal point for her interactions with Kong.

but what of the relationship between Ann and Kong?

Whenever possible, Andy has placed himself where Kong's head will be: "I can be twenty, forty feet away, up on top of a scissor lift. But it's very important, although we can't physically touch each other, that we're inside each other's head space and that it gives her something that is real, living, and playing acting decisions with her, so she doesn't have to just look up, pretend that someone's there, and drive her own emotions. She can respond to what I'm doing."

"Thank goodness for Andy," says Naomi. "He can really transport me to a whole other place. I'm not looking at him wearing a funny suit. I'm looking at him with all this behavior and all this feeling, and I can't imagine who else could make me feel the way he's making me feel. It's really something."

For Andy, however, this is just the first stage of creating Kong. Once principal photography wraps, he'll launch into months of motion-capture work, creating the performance that will drive the digital version of Kong. Naomi won't be there; she's way too big to interact physically with an Andy-sized Kong.

Which is why Andy's work on set is as much for Kong as it is for Ann: "Having lived through the scenes with Naomi, when I come to play them on my own without anybody there for nine weeks, I will have encoded into my muscles and my brain what each scene is about.

"There are so many different departments, all looking at their own particular thing: the survey department looking at the landscape, the camera department looking at the shots. With no actual Kong on set, it would be easy to lose sight of his performance. My job is to be the guardian of the character through the entire process."

Going Ape

Andy Serkis wears a black gorilla suit when he plays Kong on set. "It's his wardrobe," says first assistant director Carolynne Cunningham. "He has a set of gorilla hands, and he has this gorilla body thing which Howard Berger from KNB Effects loaned us, and he's got this head like a gorilla's head. And it really transforms him and it makes a lot of difference. It makes you perceive him more as a gorilla than an actor playing a gorilla.

"The first time it came out, we all laughed, but after that we kind of got the point. I used to take him for walks in his little suit. He'd grab my hand. It was hysterical."

To many of his fellow actors, Andy appeared as Kong for the first time on the enormous Mount Crawford set—the gates to the jungle. Until then, most had only seen him playing his other role, Lumpy the cook.

"All of a sudden," recalls Colin Hanks, "he sort of pops up, and he starts going apeshit. And we're all in the moment, and he is freaking me out. I mean, he's a gorilla—albeit he's not a twenty-five-foot gorilla."

"I was so scared," says Jack Black. "He is so insane as King Kong. He is not a human. I was looking into the eyes of an insane beast!"

Andy Serkis on the motion capture stage in a Kong mocap suit.

As principal photography wraps, New York is dismantled, costumes are boxed, and his fellow actors head back to their home countries, Andy Serkis is beginning nine weeks of grueling mocap (motion-capture) work.

In a big tin shed, just a stone's throw away from Weta Digital and Park Road Post, Andy is lying down, simulating Kong sleeping. One arm is outflung, one hand cradled gently at his chest. No rocky lair or jungle of roots and vines here: the set for today's scenes is a thick rubber mat, a couple of bare wooden risers, and a motley collection of benches and stools.

His leading lady is a disheveled Barbie doll. His costume is a blue-and-black, figure-hugging body-suit, bulked out by padded knees, elbows, gloves, and head-gear. A thick wad of foam padding rounds out his belly. Heavy weights are strapped to his arms, thighs, and ankles, to give his movements the momentum of a larger, heavier creature. In his mouth is a set of fake Kong teeth, and a microphone is taped to one cheek. He is dotted all over with silver spots.

Around and above him are dazzling pinpoints of light from many small spot-lights, each with a tiny camera next to it. Bundles of cables snake across the floor to a row of tables sporting a collection of lap-tops, keyboards, and monitors. One moni-tor shows footage of Adrien Brody as Jack,

creeping into Kong's lair. Another shows previz (previsualization animation) of Kong waking, setting Ann onto a ledge out of harm's way, and attacking Jack.

A third monitor shows a split-screen image of Andy and Kong. Both figures are in the low-resolution, blocky style of a pre-viz animation. They are digital puppets, one man-shaped, one gorilla-shaped, both imitating the real Andy. As Andy stands, so do the puppets.

It's all done with mirrors, says Matt Madden from Giant Studios, which owns the motion-capture tech-nology. He points to Andy's silver spots. "Those markers are placed on locations that best represent how his body is moving. The sil-very material is made up of a bunch of tiny little mirrors. It's the same material you see in street signs and running shoes. Our cameras have a light that shines down on those mirrors, the reflected light is shone back into the camera, the camera re-lays that information to the computer, and the computer does a 3D reconstruction in virtual space."

Andy leans forward and dangles his arms so that his knuckles rest on a low bench set up in front of him. The digital Andy puppet follows the move exactly, but the Kong puppet, with its longer arms, drops down onto all fours.

"The computer replica of Andy's body knows which of Andy's bones each marker

MOTION CAPTURE

Andy Serkis physically acts out Kong's movements in conjunction with digital animation on screen behind him.

82

is on and where it is on that bone," says Matt. "Then we have the Kong character, which has different bone lengths. Our job is to define how Andy's motion should look on Kong and make that offset."

"The movements are one-to-one down as far as my waist," says Andy. "My legs are foreshortened on the Kong puppet, so they're really where my knees are. Getting used to locomotion like that is very weird."

The knee-high benches help. They have been strategically positioned as higher ground for Andy's hands, to allow him to move as if he too were on all fours. Foam cubes stand in for some rocks to be tossed aside, and foam squabs have been gaffer-taped to the benches at specific points he needs to thump, as Kong attempting to crush Jack.

Previz of the scene provides the mocap team with a clear guide to Kong's actions and the layout of his lair. During principal photography, survey cameras mapped the live-action sets so that they could be reproduced on computer. "We know exactly what the ground plan is that we're working to," says Andy, "and it's very, very precise."

Despite the detailed preplanning, there is still room for Andy to develop Kong's performance: "The other day, we were trying to find a way of Kong looking at Ann. It's a private moment, and he knows he feels connected to her. He was supposed to just have

her in his hand, and it's supposed to be quite a still scene. But eventually we found that a more physicalized version of the scene, where he starts to cradle her, he's not looking at her and he's slightly rocking, actually conveyed a lot more about what he felt."

Andy had hesitated when Peter Jackson first asked him to play Kong. At the time, he was working on *The Lord of the Rings*, crawling around the motion-capture stage as Gollum, the computer-generated character hailed throughout the film industry as a breakthrough in CG animation.

"It was scary to go into another computer-generated character straight after Gollum," admits Andy. "But then Pete and Fran talked about where they wanted to go with the characterization. I became very excited about making him a creature that was driven by an actor's choices, although finally manifested in CG."

Andy and previsualization director/animation director Christian Rivers have talked through a sequence of action that will have Kong interacting with Ann and Jack when layered into the live-action footage. Andy performs the choreography. He wallops the benches and slashes at the foam cubes, sending them flying. His motion is swift, but his arms move with a heavy swing and there's an exaggerated bounce to his shoulders and head after each impact. Despite his too long legs, his too short arms, and his silver spots, he somehow, amazingly, looks like a gorilla.

"Gorillas have very swayed backs and very heavy bellies, so I'm bent and my bum is in the air for quite a lot of the time," he says. "I'm knuckle-walking. Gorillas use their knuckles to walk on. Sometimes we use arm extensions and put motion-capture dots on them, and that's fine if I'm just traveling, but not if I need to use my hands. They've got thick shoulder and neck muscles, so my head's slightly drooped below the shoulders. They've got a broad, bandy gait in the back legs. I've got huge weights on my fore-arms, across my thighs, and on my ankles, so that every movement has a momentum to it, because Kong is twenty-five feet tall. Not only does motion capture pick up shapes that you're doing, but it picks up impact and any incidental movement, any cough or breathing. It's a fantastically truthful tool."

For the last take of the day, Andy is given permission to go crazy. He roars. He thrashes. He thumps, swipes, and pounds. Christian Rivers screams at him, "They're attacking Ann! You're looking around for a place to put Ann! You put her in a safe place. They're attacking *you!* They're on your back!"

Andy falls onto his back and rolls frantically. He claws at his face, like a creature insane with pain and anger. It's as if he's caught up in a violent nightmare, swarmed by a mass of vicious bugs of his own imagining. The attack dies down. He pulls himself up to his full height, opens his mouth wide, beats his chest, and lets out a mighty roar. Then he collapses in a rag-doll heap onto a crash mat behind him.

Nobody else has breathed for the past two minutes. The motion-capture crew lets out a collective sigh and bursts into a spontaneous round of applause.

Peter Jackson, Naomi Watts, and Andy Serkis on set.

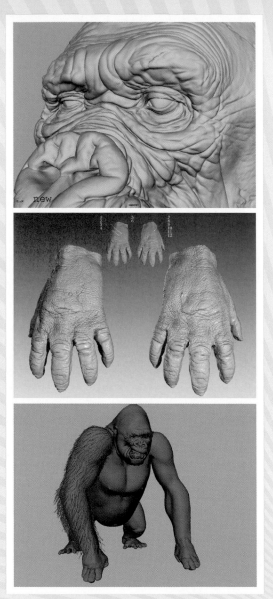

Top: Detail of Kong's facial geometry. Middle: Kong hand models. Bottom: Kong fur dynamic simulation.

Gollum was one of Weta Digital's greatest achievements during the making of *The Lord of the Rings* trilogy. The digital character impressed audiences and visual effects professionals alike. His motion-capture-led animation made for a memorable performance, which was made all the more believable by the astonishingly lifelike look of his skin.

"It was such an important breakthrough for us to figure out what makes skin look like skin—especially human skin," says *King Kong* senior visual effects supervisor Joe Letteri. "We created a technique called subsurface scattering to simulate translucency in the skin."

"Your face is not a flat color," explains Richard Taylor. "Light is passing through seven layers of corpuscles and then re reflecting back out of the skin, giving a translucent effect. If I open my mouth, my mouth is not black. The inside of my nostrils are not black. They glow subtly with a pinkish glow, because light is penetrating the subsurface of my skin and then scattering, and it is that technique which we had been pursuing for many years.

"Joe Letteri saw a silicone puppet that Gino Acevedo had painted where all of our paint was added as a surface on top of the silicone, but still generated the impression of subsurface scattering. Gino is a totally traditional artist. Combine his skills

with digital artists and, in a matter of four months, we found a cohesive crossover that allowed us to come up with the technology that made Gollum's skin look real."

Weta Digital now applies that illusion of translucency to every creature they create: "No matter how tough or hidebound the skin, it is still skin," says Joe. "Just getting a little bit of that quality into the skin helps bring it that much more alive. Even Kong, under all the fur, and as old and scarred as he is, when you do see his skin, it still has to look like a real creature."

With Kong's fur, the visual effects team is moving beyond Gollum. "We've seen fur done very well in the past," says Joe. "What we're trying to do now is bring that life of the skin that we had in Gollum to the way we create fur. Some of those same properties are what makes hair or fur look as it does. It's really hard to put your finger on it and get the look of it right. There's a translucency to hair that we're trying to capture. And that'll work for any of the digital doubles that we have to create, as well as for the big guy."

For seven months now, a digital effects team has been totally engrossed in creating Kong's fur and skin. "We've got three guys doing fur," says Guy Williams, Kong CG supervisor. "One guy's doing the

DIGITAL FUR AND SKIN

Kong fur in a work-in-progress stage.

Kong head fur in a work-in-progress stage.

legs, one's doing the back and the arms, and the other's doing the head. And we've got six guys doing textures, two or three writing shaders, which describe how surfaces should respond to light. We've been working on Kong since the dawn of time!" He laughs.

"Not just the fur—the whole look of Kong. He's been various different apes over time."

Guy delves into his computer and brings up video footage of an albino gorilla with an extraordinarily mobile and expressive face. "This is an ape by the name of Snowflake. Fran and Pete went to a zoo in Spain and spent a day looking at it and videotaping it. Snowflake was the only albino ape in captivity—spectacular-looking creature. Unfortunately he's passed away now. Pete initially loved the look of the character of Snowflake, because the skin on Snowflake was very baggy, very saggy. The face was almost human-looking—really baggy eyes and tons of folds in the face, and he seems to have a lot more range of expression in his face than other apes. So that was one of the main original designs with

Kong . . . and that's also one of the things that we're stepping back on now.

"Our second generation of Kong doesn't have half as many bags in the cheek region, and the brow is incredibly smooth compared to what Snowflake had, but there's still a lot of character there. Fran and animation want to maintain the ability to see the expression in Kong's eyes, so we're reducing the size of the brow back so they won't be so shadowed. Obviously Kong was never going to be an albino ape. We went towards gray-brown fur, and then it was decided that Kong was going to be a black ape, with white fur. It's a constant refinement process."

Kong needs to look like a real gorilla, but he also needs to look gargantuan—and it's not a matter of simply scaling him up. "We keep pinning a little Naomi Watts cutout in there beside Kong, just so you can get a sense of the scale," says Guy. "With the really coarse hair on an ape, by the time you scale it up so he's twenty-five feet tall, it would be a millimeter in width. So then, when you've got Naomi running her hands over it, it's not like she's running her hands through hair, it's like she's rubbing her hands through spaghetti. But if you take a twenty-five-feet tall gorilla and put normal hair on it, it will look like a really soft plush toy, because the hair is too fine now in relationship to the size of the ape. That's one of the big things we keep waffling back and forth on—the width and the number of hairs. It's this weird scale thing that we keep chasing."

The color of Kong's eyes is also up for tweaking. "Real apes have a variety of different eyes. It's bizarre. Humans always have a white sclera area and a colored iris. We've got pictures of apes that have a black sclera and black iris, but we've seen some that have a deep creamy brown sclera with a really black iris. So we're trying to figure out which is the best-looking one. I'm leaning more towards darker myself, for the simple reason that you don't look at that and think there's a guy in an ape suit."

Having a twenty-five-foot Kong interacting with a normal-sized Naomi Watts means that he must be ultradetailed and extremely high resolution. "Whenever you see Naomi inside the digital Kong's hand, his thumb will be really large in frame," says Guy. "Kong is about four times the resolution of Gollum. We have to get a lot closer to parts of Kong than we ever had to on Gollum. We've painted all the pores on the skin, the really fine wrinkles, and we actually painted all the fingerprints, including on the palms and the thumb. That snaggletooth is about a foot and a half tall, and Naomi is going to be standing next to Kong's face a lot, so you're going to see that tooth jutting out. You wouldn't think a tooth would need so much detail." He laughs.

The good news is that the digital artists don't have to repaint all those details for each and every shot: "Once we've painted those maps, they're available—they never have to change. So we painted the fingerprints for his hand and we'll never paint them again."

The latest version of Kong's skin shows a shift from a leathery elephant-hide look to a more apelike, black, polished leather. "It's kind of cool," says Guy. "It looks like a fancy horse.

"One of Pete's constant driving factors is that Kong is an old ape and he has not lived a happy life. Everything wants to kill him and he doesn't really mind killing it back, so he's covered in all these really beautiful scars. We've been trying to get the character of those down. We have hero scars, where we'll cut the fur out in those areas. Other scars we might only see through the hair."

The Kong team has developed a series of texture maps that govern the behavior of Kong's skin, telling it where to be leathery, where it flexes more, where it is shiny, where dull or dirty, where moist. The skin on

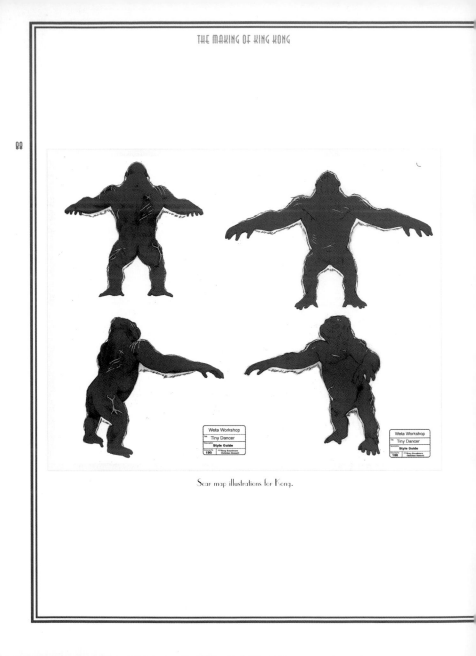

Scar map illustrations for Kong.

the back of the fingers will be more dull and leathery, the skin on the face more shiny and flexible, with wetness under the eyes and on the lips. The degree of subsurface scattering can be dialed up or down for greater translucency in the skin of the face, less in the skin of dusty hands.

Weta Digital's fur software was originally written for the digital doubles on *The Lord of the Rings*. "Basically, it detects a surface and you tell it to grow fur," says Guy. "Then we have to tell the fur how to behave once it comes off the surface– to wave around a little, for example, or to group into bigger clumps of fur. The amount of effort that goes into the creation of the fur is just staggering. Right now it still has a unifor-

mity to it. We're fighting to get it to look more organic.

"Kong has hairs on his arm that are over four feet long. It's like a horse's mane, but we don't want to make it as floppy as a horse's tail and we don't want to make it too stiff." Then there's getting the hair to move naturally in the wind, flicker with the impact of Kong's hands or feet hitting the ground, respond appropriately to light, with a peppering of white hairs among the black, and maybe some reddish highlights but not so much that he will turn red from the subsurface scattering of New York's dawn light . . . "One of the fun things about working in a place like this is that there is no end to the attention to detail," Guy says with a grin.

Final shot of Kong fur.

Kong in his final moments.

When Peter Jackson, as a child growing up in New Zealand, first attempted to film *King Kong*'s Empire State Building sequence, his special effects techniques were not so very different from those used in the original *King Kong*.

Young Peter built a model of the Empire State Building and a simple stop-motion Kong and painted a bedsheet with a Manhattan skyline to pin up as a background. For the 1933 movie, a stop-motion Kong climbed a model Empire State Building in front of a sheet of glass with skyscrapers painted on it and, behind that, a painted backdrop of the Hudson River and shoreline. A small doll stood in for actress Fay Wray in the wider shots, and model biplanes circled Kong on wires. For closer shots of Ann, live-action shots of Fay Wray were back projected onto a tiny screen positioned within the miniature setting.

THE TRAGIC END

Amost seventy years later, with a wealth of cutting-edge digital technology at his fingertips, the challenge for Peter is to create an Empire State Building sequence that will be as good as the original.

When *King Kong* came out in 1933, with its thrilling climactic scenes on top of the Empire State Building, the movie immediately found favor with audiences. "It was a smash success," says Peter. "It was the equivalent of *Star Wars* or *Jurassic Park*. It was audacious and outra-geous . . . a brilliant piece of storytelling."

The shock of the new made the film's final scenes especially powerful. "In 1933," says senior visual effects supervisor Joe Letteri, "the idea of seeing this big gorilla from the other side of the world was not a common thing. Mountain gorillas had only been discovered some thirty years before that, so these were big, unknown, almost mythological wild creatures at that time. . . .

"At the same time, we had the brand-new Empire State Building, which had just opened. Most people had never left the ground. Air travel and going up into very tall buildings wasn't common. So one of the brilliant things that the original *King Kong* did was it brought both of those worlds together. You have this beast that was king of his jungle lair come to the heart of civilization and rise to the top of the tallest building in the world, where you see this incredible vista. Those images were stunning and had a big effect on audiences at the time."

These days, wild creatures, airplane flights, and sweeping views from high places are not such a big deal. "We've all taken an elevator to the top of the Empire State Building, or we've seen photos," says Joe. "We take spectacular vistas for granted. We're so used to air travel being a comfortable thing for us. But if you climb into one of those biplanes, you realize

Previz for Curtiss HellDivers' attack on Kong at the Empire State Building.

there's not much between you and the ground but a little bit of wood."

In faithfully re-creating an authentic 1930s cityscape—New York as today's audiences have never seen it—the visual effects team at Weta Digital is hoping to give audiences a glimmer of what 1930s audiences must have felt when they saw the Empire State Building sequence for the first time. "We wanted to bring people back to that era, when that clash of the two worlds was just happening for the first time," says Joe. "That's really the power of the story—this magnificent creature that is the last of his kind meeting civilization at its pinnacle. We're hoping to bring to audiences that sense of 'Wow, this is really amazing.'"

In Weta's digital New York, with the city's skyscrapers pared down to 1930s heights, the Empire State Building regains its stature as the tallest building in the world. "The Empire State Building is so much taller than anything else on the entire island," says Peter. "It stands out right in the middle like this huge needle. It's quite striking."

For Peter, making *King Kong* is the opportunity of a lifetime to re-create an iconic cinematic image for a new generation of filmgoers. "That black-and-white photograph of Kong on the Empire State Building swatting at planes, that's been in every book about the history of film that's been published in the last seventy years. By re-creating it we're tipping our hat towards an historic film moment."

Re-creating the sequence does not mean sticking slavishly to the original. The stop-motion Kong and two-dimensional painted backdrops of the 1933 movie constrained the pioneer filmmakers to static shots with the camera locked in selected positions, but Peter has a three-dimensional digital city and a digital Kong to play with.

"I'm able to do what they couldn't do in 1933, which is to move the camera around a whole lot more, and to have a lot more freedom with the camera angles. You've got aeroplanes wheeling and diving and swooping around the building, and I've used that a lot in the camera angles to try and give a very vertiginous and highly exhilarated version of the sequence."

A visit to the real Empire State Building, early in preproduction, kick-started the replicating of it for the movie. "We walked through it, measuring and photographing it," says production designer Grant Major. "We went to the upper observation deck, which is at the very top of the building, then climbed up above the observation deck to the machine level at the very top of the cone, and then went through a trapdoor and stood on the very, very top of the cone, as Ann did in the original film. At six o'clock on a fine New York day, it was freezing cold and very windy. It's not a very people-friendly place up there."

Structurally, the building is the same as it was when it was first built, but there have been many cosmetic changes. The very top of the building was originally intended to be an airport for dirigibles such as the ill-fated *Hindenburg*, with the upper observation deck conceived as a reception lounge for passengers, and what is now a television mast designed as a mooring mast for the airships, but that plan was scuttled by the high winds. "It's just a sea of microwave stations and radio masts up there now," says Grant. "Back then, it was quite a clean art deco shape. Fortunately, there's a quantity of archival photographs and movie footage of the time, so it's quite well recorded."

Most of the building as seen in the 2005 movie is a digital re-creation, but several small areas have been reproduced as physical sets. They include the entrance lobby, observation decks, stairways, exterior walkway and ladders, and, of course, the very tip of the cone where Kong fights the biplanes. "They're all completely different sets, and they're all based exactly one-to-one scale on the architectural drawings, measurements, and archival photographs of the Empire State Building," says Grant.

Some of the sets feature in the briefest of shots, yet have still been created with great attention to detail. For example, a lobby was built so that Adrien Brody, as Jack, could run through it and into the elevator. The lobby took weeks to paint because its wooden floor needed to look like marble.

"We had eight people painting it for around six weeks, full-time," says set finishing supervisor Kathryn Lim. "There are thirteen steps to painting marble. Every single step has to be sanded, because you want to have a mirror finish on it and it needs to look like it's got a lot of depth, that it is a beautiful organic piece of stone. There's a lot of blood, sweat, and tears that's gone into that marble."

The set for the top piece of the Empire State Building, the roof of the mast, was just a few meters across and set against a blue-screen background. It was built of medium-density fiberboard, prepacked

with plugged-up bullet holes, plastered over, and painted to give it a smooth metal finish with not a bullet hole in sight. Between shots, the plugs could be popped out to reveal the holes.

Many of the bullet hits and ricochet effects on the building will be digital, but some strikes, such as those around Ann on the ladder, were created by the special effects team. "In reality," says Steve Ingram, special effects coordinator, "bullets going in just make a hole. But, in the film world, all bullet hits project outwards because visually the public expect more out of it. We put a squib, a little detonator, in the bullet hole, then we fill the hole with a mix of plasticine and silver dust. When you set the squib off, it blows out soft pieces that look like little shreds of metal but won't hurt anyone."

Shards of flying glass will be digital effects, but for some scenes the special effects team has made actor-friendly fake glass. "We made silicone glass which looks really real," says Steve. "You can crumble it with your fingers. It's for putting on actors. It doesn't matter if it falls down your sleeve or collar."

When Naomi Watts played Ann Darrow's final emotion-packed moments with the dying Kong, she was sitting on the tiniest of sets, surrounded by the film crew and a clutter of filmmaking paraphernalia. Stunt performers poked at her with huge blue-screened sausages, standing in for Kong's big, black, furry fingers. Andy Serkis stood above her on a snorkel lift, wearing a gorilla suit of sorts and grunting through the Kongalizer.

The biplanes were shot against blue screens in a separate studio. They juddered around on motion rigs, while a film light, standing in for the sun, swung past on a crane to give an impression of greater movement.

The completed Empire State Building sequence will involve a complex mixing and matching of live-

Curtiss Helldiver digital model.

An early frame from the Helldiver sequence.

action sets within a digital building, live-action and digital biplanes, special effects and digital destruction, live-action scenes shot out at the Seaview set, a vast digital city, a Wellington sky, actors, stunt doubles, digital doubles, and a digital Kong based on Andy's motion-captured performance. With computer wizardry, all the separate elements will seamlessly be woven together.

"The technology today is so incredible," says Peter. "Anything that you imagine is now possible on film. Anything that you want to see, you can create in the computer. In some respects, it is simpler to make movies now than it was ten years ago, because you're not grappling with the 'How do I do that?' factor—which is good because I think that what's important now is to go back to the story and the characters."

Ultimately, of course, the Empire State Building sequence is not about bullet holes, blue sausage fingers, and digital buildings. It is about a wild creature trapped in a hostile alien world, an actress who is desperate to save him, a writer finding the courage to say that he loves her, and a filmmaker's reckless, shattered ambition. It is about Kong fighting the biplanes high above New York City, and the tragic bond between two lonely souls.

ACKNOWLEDGMENTS

Thanks to:

Peter Jackson.

Gino Acevedo, Matt Aitken, Judy Alley, Jon Allitt, Malcolm Angell, John Baster, Jeremy Bennett, Danielle Birch, David Birrell, Jan Blenkin, Melissa Booth, Philippa Boyens, Greg Broadmore, Jed Brophy, Andrew Calder, Cindy Chang, Tanea Chapman, Julie Chebbi, Carolynne Cunningham, Gene DeMarco, Jason Docherty, Tony Drawbridge, Eddie Egan, Bette Einbinder, Ryk Fortuna, Richard Frances-Moore, Alex Funke, Eliza Godman, Dave Goodin, Beth Goss, Simon Hames, Ben Hawker, Jennifer Heddle, Chris Hennah, Dan Hennah, Belindalee Hope, Mike Hopkins, Gray Horsfield, Christopher Horvath, Bill Hunt, Gus Hunter, Steve Ingram, Helen Jorda, Peter King, Eric Leighton, Dan Lemmon, Joe Letteri, Kathryn Lim, Simon Lowe, Matt Madden, Grant Major, Clothilde Mayer, Sarah Milnes, Cynthia Modders, Eileen Moran, Ed Mulholland, Gayle Munro, Jabez Olssen, Phred Palmer, Christian Pearce, Hammond Peek, Dana Peters, Christian Rivers, Terry Ryan, Eric Saindon, Jennifer Sandberg, Atsushi Sato, Jamie Selkirk, Andy Serkis, Scott Shannon, Ben Snow, Chris Streeter, Amy Taylor, Richard Taylor, Ethan Van der Ryn, Paul Van Ommen, Ra Vincent, Nick Weir, Chris White, Fraser Wilkinson, Guy Williams, Jamie Wilson, Erik Winquist, Ben Wootten, Jake Yocum.